Extremism And Reformation

David Myatt

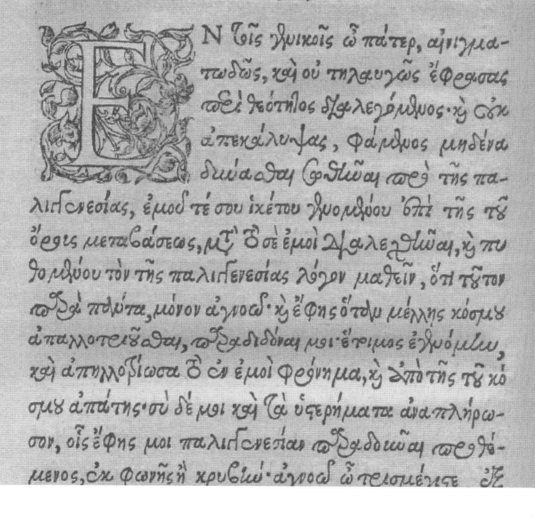

Contents

Preface

The genesis of this compilation of essays was, as mentioned in the included essay *A Premature Grieving*, the publication in 2019, by political advocacy group, of various unsubstantiated allegations and disinformation about me and the subsequent repetition of such allegations and disinformation by some mainstream newspapers and media outlets.

The unsubstantiated allegations and the disinformation concerned my supposed continuing involvement with extremism, specifically neo-nazism; it being apparent that neither the political advocacy group nor the newspapers and media which repeated the allegations and the disinformation had bothered to read my extensive post-2011 writings about rejecting extremism and about seeking expiation for my decades-long extremist past [1].

This compilation of essays is my reply to those unsubstantiated allegations and disinformation.

While two of the essays included in this compilation - both written in 2012 and respectively titled *Concerning Some Abstractions* and *Some Notes on The Politics and Ideology of Hate* - have been superseded by my 2013 book *Understanding And Rejecting Extremism* [2] and by subsequent writings concerning the 'philosophy of pathei-mathos' they nevertheless in my fallible view may have some relevance for those interested both in my rejection of extremism and how and why I developed my 'numinous way' into my post-2012 'philosophy of pathei-mathos'. [3]

For the writing of those two essays - with their assuredness, their many suppositions, their many generalizations and some rhetoric - helped me organize and then refine my thoughts about extremism in general and my own extremist past in particular. It also made me moderate both my thoughts and how I came to express those thoughts in writing; a moderation expressed by my *Understanding And Rejecting Extremism.*

In a similar way, my 2012 essay *Some Philosophical and Moral Problems of National-Socialism*, [4] also included in this compilation, helped me organize and then express in writing my thoughts about National Socialism and Hitler.

It should be noted that many of the texts referenced in the older essays included in this compilation - many referencing my now dated 'numinous way' - are available only in archived versions of my website and weblog, [5] having been replaced, post-2012, by my writings concerning the philosophy of pathei-mathos, about which philosophy I have included as an appendix here my recent text *Physis And Being: An Introduction To The Philosophy Of Pathei-Mathos.*

I have reproduced the essays as they were originally published even though there is some repetition of content and/or of quotations between some of the included essays.

The illustration is the beginning of the Greek text of tractate XIII of the Corpus Hermeticum from the book *Mercvrii Trismegisti Pœmandres*, published in Paris in 1554.

My translation is:

> When, father, you in the Exoterica conversed about divinity your language was enigmatic and obscure. There was, from you, no disclosure; instead, you said no one can be rescued before the Palingenesis. Now, following our discussion as we were passing over the mountain I became your supplicant, inquiring into learning the discourse on Palingenesis since that, out of all of them, is the only one unknown to me, with you saying it would be imparted to me when I became separated from the world.
>
> Thus I prepared myself, distancing my ethos from the treachery in the world. [6]

David Myatt
September 2019
Third Edition

°°°

[1] On the question of expiation, qv. my essay *Numinous Expiation* written in 2012 and included in *Religion, Empathy, and Pathei-Mathos* (International Standard Book Number 978-1484097984).

As I wrote in *Some Questions For DWM* (March 2014),

> "In a very personal sense, my philosophy of pathei-mathos is expiative, as are my writings concerning extremism, such as my *Understanding and Rejecting Extremism: A Very Strange Peregrination.*

[2] International Standard Book Number 978-1484854266.

[3] The essay *Concerning The Development Of The Numinous Way* outlines the change from 'the numinous way' to the philosophy of pathei-mathos. It is available at https://davidmyatt.wordpress.com/rejecting-extremism

/development-of-the-numinous-way/

[4] An archive version of the essay is available at https://web.archive.org /web/20130509183014/http://davidmyatt.wordpress.com/moral-problems-of-national-socialism/

[5] See for example: (i) https://web.archive.org/web/20130602171008/http: //davidmyatt.wordpress.com/ and (ii) https://web.archive.org/web/20130704131205/http://www.davidmyatt.info/

[6] David Myatt, *Eight Tractates*, 2017, International Standard Book Number 978-1976452369

A Premature Grieving

A recent occurrence, although expected for some years, saddened me expressing as it seemed to do something about our human physis; about how for so many people our physis does not seem to have evolved that much, if at all, despite our thousands of years old human culture of pathei-mathos.

The occurrence was the publication of a report, in two parts of which report I was repeatedly mentioned, with the author of those parts making various allegations about me for which he provided no evidence; who misattributed certain quotations to me; who made fundamental and multiple factual errors; who committed various logical fallacies; who was generally biased and dishonourable and who thus rather than promoting hope and fairness promoted old-world hostility toward and a stereotyping of particular individuals.

My resigned sadness was because for that author it was as if propaganda on behalf of some cause came before, was more important than, truth and empathy; as if there was for that author no personal belief in redemption, in the possibility of individuals changing for the better, except insofar – perchance – as such change was toward the cause he believed in; and thus as if the author was selective, judgemental, about those given the benefit of the doubt using the ideology of some cause, or their own prejudice, rather than humanity, as the criteria of judgement.

As I wrote in 2012:

> "could my career as an extremist have been brought to an earlier end had one or some of my opponents taken the trouble to get to know me

personally and rationally revealed to me the error of my suffering-causing, unethical, extremist ways? Perhaps; perhaps not – I admit I do not know. I do know, however, how my personal interaction with, and the ethical behaviour of, the Police I interacted with from the time of my arrest by officers from SO12 in 1998, permanently changed (for the better) my attitude toward the Police." [1]

Instead of an empathic, a human, an honourable approach the author preferred propaganda, repeating the stereotyping he used almost two decades ago. Thus my extensive writings in the past eight years about rejecting all forms of extremism, my extensive and intensely personal writings regarding my struggle to reform myself as a result of pathei-mathos, were ignored. [2]

"Thus am I humbled, once more, by such knowing feeling of the burden made from my so heavy past; so many errors, mistakes. So many to humble me here, now, by such profusion as becomes prehension of centuries past and passing, bringing as such a passing does such gifts of they now long beyond life's ending who crafted from faith, feeling, experience, living, love, those so rich presents replete with meaning; presenting thus to us if only for a moment – fleeting as Thrush there feeding – that knowing of ourselves as beings who by empathy, life, gifts, and love, can cease to be some cause of suffering.

For no longer is there such a need – never was there such a need – to cause such suffering as we, especially I, have caused. For are not we thinking thoughtful beings – possessed of the numinous will to love?

But my words, my words – so unlike such musick [Dunstable: Preco preheminencie] – fail: such finite insubstantial things; such a weak conduit for that flowing of wordless feeling that, as such musick, betakes us far out beyond our causal selves to where we are, can be, should be, must be, the non-interfering beauty of a moment; a sublime life seeking only to so gently express that so gentle love that so much faith has sometimes so vainly so tried to capture, express, and manifest; as when that boyish man as monk past Compline knelt in gentleness to feel to become such peace, such a human happiness, as so many others have felt centuries past and present, one moment flowing so numinously to another." [3]

Yet, as I wrote some years ago,

"I harbour no resentment against individuals, or organizations, or groups, who over the past forty or so years have publicly and/or privately made negative or derogatory comments about me or published items making claims about me.

Indeed, I now find myself in the rather curious situation of not only agreeing with some of my former political opponents on many matters, but also (perhaps) of understanding (and empathizing with) their motivation; a situation which led and which leads me to appreciate even more just how lamentable my extremism was and just how arrogant, selfish, wrong, and reprehensible, I as a person was, and how in many ways many of those former opponents were and are (ex concesso) better people than I ever was or am.

Which is one reason why I have written what I have recently written about extremism and my extremist past: so that perchance someone or some many may understand extremism, and its causes, better and thus be able to avoid the mistakes I made, avoid causing the suffering I caused; or be able to in some way more effectively counter or prevent such extremism in the future. And one reason – only one – why I henceforward must live in reclusion and *in silencio.*" [4]

That I have now broken such self-imposed silence is the result of my resigned sadness regarding how far we mortals still have to travel to be able to live, en masse, empathic and compassionate lives, and of how so many individuals still – from whatever personal motive or because of some cause or ideology – promote old-world hostility toward and a stereotyping of particular individuals.

Perhaps the goddess Δίκη will touch some of those so many hostile individuals, for as Aeschylus wrote,

Δίκα δὲ τοῖς μὲν παθοῦσιν μαθεῖν ἐπιρρέπει:
τὸ μέλλον δ᾽, ἐπεὶ γένοιτ᾽, ἂν κλύοις: πρὸ χαιρέτω:
ἴσον δὲ τῷ προστένειν.

"Δίκη favours someone learning from adversity:
But I shall hear of what will be, after it comes into being:
Before then, I leave it,
Otherwise, it is the same as a premature grieving." [5]

Which is yet one more reason why I am still learning and still have far to travel, for that recent occurrence brought a premature grieving.

Ash Wednesday 2019

[1] *A Matter of Honour*, 2012.

[2] These writings include (i) *Just My Fallible Views, Again,* (ii) *Understanding and Rejecting Extremism* (pdf), (iii) *Religion, Empathy, and Pathei-Mathos* (pdf), and the letters and essays included in (iv) *Such Respectful Wordful Offerings* (pdf).

[3] *Bright Berries, One Winter,* written 22 December 2010.

[4] *Pathei-Mathos – Genesis of My Unknowing*, written in 2012.

[5] Agamemnon, 250-253.

A Perplexing Failure To Understand

Being a slightly revised extract from a letter to friend,
with some footnotes added post scriptum

One of the multitude of things that I have, for years, failed to understand – sans any belief in an all-powerful supra-personal deity – is why I am still alive while people like Sue and Fran – and the millions of others like them – died or were killed, too early. For they neither caused any deaths nor inflicted any suffering on another living being, human and otherwise, while I – and the millions like me, worldwide – continued to live despite having so caused, directly and/or indirectly, deaths and suffering. And in my case, directly and indirectly as my documented so lamentable extremist amoral decades – of violence, hatred, incitement, of being a "theoretician of revolution/terror" – so clearly reveal.

Yet – over twenty years after the death of Sue, and almost ten years since the death of Fran – here I am, still breathing, still pontificating. And all I have – despite years of interior reflexion – is a feeling, an intuition: of the how and why our thousand of years old human culture of pathei-mathos is important because – or so it seems to me – it might bring (at least to some others) a wordless intimation of one possible answer to such a perplexing question.

For it is a culture that includes, for example, such diverse artisements as the Oresteia of Aeschylus, the *Lamentations of Jeremiah* by Thomas Tallis, and the life – and death – of people such as Jesse James, Mohandas K Gandhi, and Edith Cavell; and which culture, enshrined as it is in Studia Humanitatis, can perchance teach some of each new generation that valuable lesson about our human physis, jumelle as our physis is [1] and thus paradoxical as we honourable/dishonourable (often hubriatic) mortals are:

> ἄνδρα μοι ἔννεπε, μοῦσα, πολύτροπον, ὃς μάλα πολλὰ
> πλάγχθη, ἐπεὶ Τροίης ἱερὸν πτολίεθρον ἔπερσεν:
> πολλῶν δ᾽ ἀνθρώπων ἴδεν ἄστεα καὶ νόον ἔγνω,
> πολλὰ δ᾽ ὅ γ᾽ ἐν πόντῳ πάθεν ἄλγεα ὃν κατὰ θυμόν,
> ἀρνύμενος ἥν τε ψυχὴν καὶ νόστον ἑταίρων.
> ἀλλ᾽ οὐδ᾽ ὣς ἑτάρους ἐρρύσατο, ἱέμενός περ:
> αὐτῶν γὰρ σφετέρῃσιν ἀτασθαλίῃσιν ὄλοντο,
> νήπιοι, οἳ κατὰ βοῦς Ὑπερίονος Ἠελίοιο
> ἤσθιον: αὐτὰρ ὁ τοῖσιν ἀφείλετο νόστιμον ἦμαρ

The Muse shall tell of the many adventures of that man
Of the many stratagems
Who, after the pillage of that hallowed citadel at Troy,
Saw the towns of many a people and experienced their ways:
He whose vigour, at sea, was weakened by many afflictions
As he strove to win life for himself and return his comrades to their
homes.
But not even he, for all this yearning, could save those comrades
For they were destroyed by their own immature foolishness
Having devoured the cattle of Helios, that son of Hyperion,
Who plucked from them the day of their returning [2]

A lesson about ourselves which so many others have attempted to communicate
to us, as recounted in a certain tragedy:

οὕτω δ᾽ Ἀτρέως παῖδας ὁ κρείσσων
ἐπ᾽ Ἀλεξάνδρῳ πέμπει ξένιος
Ζεὺς πολυάνορος ἀμφὶ γυναικὸς
πολλὰ παλαίσματα καὶ γυιοβαρῆ
γόνατος κονίαισιν ἐρειδομένου
διακναιομένης τ᾽ ἐν προτελείοις
κάμακος θήσων Δαναοῖσι
Τρωσί θ᾽ ὁμοίως. ἔστι δ᾽ ὅπη νῦν
ἔστι: τελεῖται δ᾽ ἐς τὸ πεπρωμένον

Thus were those sons of Atreus sent forth
By mighty Zeus, guardian of hospitality, against Alexander
On account of that woman who has had many men.
And many would be the limb-wearying combats
With knees pushed into the dirt
And spears worn-out in the initial sacrifice
Of Trojans and Danaans alike.
What is now, came to be
As it came to be. And its ending has been ordained [3]

and as described – millennia ago – by a certain poetess:

φαίνεταί μοι κῆνος ἴσος θέοισιν
ἔμμεν᾽ ὤνηρ, ὄττις ἐνάντιός τοι
ἰσδάνει καὶ πλάσιον ἆδυ φωνεί-
σας ὑπακούει
καὶ γελαίσας ἰμέροεν, τό μ᾽ ἦ μὰν
καρδίαν ἐν στήθεσιν ἐπτόαισεν
ὡς γὰρ ἔς σ᾽ ἴδω βρόχε᾽, ὥς με φώναι-
σ᾽ οὐδ᾽ ἒν ἔτ᾽ εἴκει,
ἀλλ᾽ ἄκαν μὲν γλῶσσα <ἔαγε>, λέπτον
δ᾽ αὔτικα χρῶι πῦρ ὑπαδεδρόμηκεν,

ὀππάτεσσι δ᾽ οὐδ᾽ ἓν ὅρημμ᾽, ἐπιρρόμ-
βεισι δ᾽ ἄκουαι,
<ἔκαδε μ᾽ ἴδρως ψῦχρος κακχέεται / κὰδ᾽ δέ ἴδρως κακχέεται>
τρόμος δὲ
παῖσαν ἄγρει, χλωροτέρα δὲ ποίας
ἔμμι, τεθνάκην δ᾽ ὀλίγω ᾽πιδεύης
φαίνομ᾽ ἔμ᾽ αὔται

I see he who sits near you as an equal of the gods
For he can closely listen to your delightful voice
And that seductive laugh
That makes the heart behind my breasts to tremble.
Even when I glimpse you for a moment
My tongue is stilled as speech deserts me
While a delicate fire is beneath my skin –
My eyes cannot see, then,
When I hear only a whirling sound
As I shivering, sweat
Because all of me trembles;
I become paler than drought-grass
And nearer to death [4]

and as, for example, described by the scribe of an ancient Hermetic MS:

Solum enim animal homo duplex est; et eius una pars simplex, quae,
ut Graeci aiunt οὐσιώδης, quam vocamus divinae similitudinis
formam; est autem quadruplex quod ὑλικὸν Graeci, nos mundanum
dicimus, e quo factum est corpus, quo circumtegitur illud quod in
homine divinum esse iam diximus, in quo mentis divinitas tecta sola
cum cognatis suis, id est mentis purae sensibus, secum ipsa
conquiescat tamquam muro corporis saepta.

Humans are the only species that is jumelle, with one aspect that
foundation which the Greeks termed οὐσιώδης and we describe as
being akin in appearance to divinity, and yet also being quadruplex,
termed by the Greeks ὑλικός and which we describe as worldly;
whereby from such is the corporeal [body] that, as mentioned, is of –
in humans – the divinity, and in which is that divine disposition, to
which it is solely related, that is in character a singular perceiveration
and untoiling since enclosed within the corporeal. [5]

But will we – can we – mortals, en masse, read, listen, reflect, experience, and
so learn? Or will we, as our tragic history of the past three millennia so seems
to indicate, continue to be divided – individually, and en masse – between the
masculous and the muliebral; between honour and dishonour; between war and
peace; between empathy and ipseity?

I do so wish I knew. But all I have to offer, now in the fading twilight of my own mortal life, is an appreciation (perhaps contrary, these days, to οἱ πλέονες) of what some schools, independent ('private') or otherwise, still fortunately do understand is the importance of a 'classical education', and of what may possibly be apprehended by such poor words of mine as these:

> Here, sea, Skylark and such a breeze as rushes reeds
> Where sandy beach meets
> To meld with sky
> And a tumbling cumuli of cloud
> Briefly cool our Sun.
>
> I am no one, while ageing memory flows:
> For was there ever such a bliss as this
> While the short night lasted
> And we touched kissed meshed ourselves together
> To sweat, sweating, humid,
> Fearing so many times to fully open our eyes
> Lest it all really was
> A dream
>
> But Dawn arrived as it then arrived bringing with its light
> Loose limbs and such a reminder
> As would could should did
> Make us late that day for work.
>
> So, here: a tiredness of age
> Brightened by such a June as this
> When sandy beach meets
> To meld with sky
> And that tumbling cumuli of cloud
> Briefly cools a Sun

For there are so many recollections of centuries of a so human love, so many memories of years – centuries – of hubris and dishonour, that I can now only live each slowly passing daylight hour modus vivendi:

> And the lost heart stiffens and rejoices
> In the lost lilac and the lost sea voices
> And the weak spirit quickens to rebel [6]

David Myatt
January 2015

[1] Pœmandres (Corpus Hermeticum), 15:

> καὶ διὰ τοῦτο παρὰ πάντα τὰ ἐπὶ γῆς ζῷα διπλοῦς ἐστιν ὁ ἄνθρωπος,
> θνητὸς μὲν διὰ τὸ σῶμα, ἀθάνατος δὲ διὰ τὸν οὐσιώδη ἄνθρωπον.

ἀθάνατος γὰρ ὢν καὶ πάντων τὴν ἐξουσίαν ἔχων τὰ θνητὰ πάσχει ὑποκείμενος τῇ εἰμαρμένῃ

Which is why, distinct among all other beings on Earth, mortals are jumelle; deathful of body yet deathless the inner mortal. Yet, although deathless and possessing full authority, the human is still subject to wyrd

See also Sophocles, Antigone, v. 334 & vv. 365-36:

πολλὰ τὰ δεινὰ κοὐδὲν ἀνθρώπου δεινότερον πέλε...
σοφόν τι τὸ μηχανόεν τέχνας ὑπὲρ ἐλπίδ᾽ ἔχων
τοτὲ μὲν κακόν, ἄλλοτ᾽ ἐπ᾽ ἐσθλὸν ἕρπει

There exists much that is strange, yet nothing
Has more strangeness than a human being...
Beyond his own hopes, his cunning
In inventive arts – he who arrives
Now with dishonour, then with chivalry

[2] Homer, Odyssey, Book 1, v. 1-9

[3] Aeschylus, Agamemnon, v. 60-68

[4] Sappho, Fragment 31

[5] Asclepius, VII, 13-20

[6] TS Eliot, Ash Wednesday

Concerning The Abstractions of Extremism and Race

In essence, I consider an abstraction to be:

"a manifestation, possibly the primary manifestation, of *the-separation-of-otherness*: of a lack of empathy, and which lack results in some distinction being made between 'them' and 'us', and thus with some living being (human or otherwise) being assigned to some abstract category, or group, and/or regarded as the genesis of or some representation of some posited existing or future ideal. Often, some abstraction – some category or some group or some ideal – is imputed to have some value, higher/lower, in relation to some other abstraction, with the result that some abstractions are considered to be 'worth fighting/killing/dying for', and/or regarded as 'morally superior' to or better than other different, or vaguely different, abstractions, even if such difference is illusory and thus only 'in the eye of the believer'." *Rejecting Abstractions - A Personal Lesson From Extremism*

There is thus a difference between an abstraction and a descriptor. A descriptor is just a word used to describe something which already exists and which is personally observed or is discovered, whereas an abstraction by its nature is: a generalization; a hypothesis; a posited thing; an assumption or assumptions about, an extrapolation of or from some-thing; or some assumed or extrapolated ideal 'form' of some-thing. Sometimes, abstractions are generalizations based on some sample(s), or on some median (average) value or sets of values, observed, sampled, or assumed.

Or expressed simply, a descriptor describes what-is as 'it' already is, according to its φύσις (physis: its nature, its being) and in accordance with wu-wei; whereas an abstraction denotes what is presumed/assumed/idealized, past or present or future. A descriptor relies on, is derived from, describes, individual knowing and individual judgement; an abstraction relies on something abstract, impersonal, such as some opinion/knowing/judgement of others or some assumptions, theory, or hypothesis made by others.

In relation to human beings, abstraction involves an assigning of individuals to some abstract category or group, and then interpreting or judging or describing those individuals according to the criteria posited for that category or group. This results in an impersonal, fallacious, presumptuous, 'knowledge' concerning those individuals, and amounts to a dehumanizing of those individuals, for a genuine knowing of them requires a personal interaction with them over a period of time and of necessity the use of the very individual faculty of empathy in the immediacy-of-the-living-moment.

Thus, as a result of such a personal knowing, an individual might be described as kind, with 'kind' being a descriptor, and neutral. As a result of using abstractions, an individual might be described as Caucasian, or as Muslim, with the abstraction, the category, Caucasian or Muslim by its nature as an abstraction imputing or conveying to others certain attributes and characteristics (of appearance, life, personality, and so on) which may or may not apply to the individual so described.

Also, and most importantly, all human manufactured abstractions ignore The Cosmic Perspective - our place in the Cosmos - and thus are a manifestation of hubris, of our arrogance, our insolence. For we human beings are simply one fragile mortal biological life-form on one planet orbiting one star in one galaxy in a Cosmos of billions of galaxies; our abstractions merely the opinionated product of our limited fallible earth-bound so-called 'intelligence', an 'intelligence', an understanding, we foolishly, arrogantly, pridefully have a tendency to believe in, have faith in, and exalt.

Extremist and Extremism

Are 'extremism' and 'extremist' abstractions? Personally I do not believe that they are, since I regard those terms as but useful descriptions of the character, the nature, of certain individuals and of their deeds; with such character and such deeds already having been revealed by the actions, by the life, of such individuals.

In effect, 'extremist' and 'extremism' are not ideals, but descriptors of what is known or revealed through observation and a personal knowing. A function of the empathic-knowing of an individual as that individual is.

As a result of some forty years of practical experience as an activist, I consider that an 'extremist' is a person who tends toward harshness, or who is harsh, or who supports/incites harshness, in pursuit of an objective that is usually considered to be of a political or of a religious nature. Hence, for me, *extremism* is the result of such harshness as well as the principles, the causes, the characteristics, that promote, incite, or describe the harsh action of extremists.

Thus, and I believe quite correctly, I have described myself - categorized myself - as an extremist, as a promoter of extremism, both during my neo-nazi years and during my years propagating a harsh interpretation of Islam, an interpretation which included supporting bin Laden and the Taliban, supporting and promoting 'martyrdom operations' ('suicide attacks' by Muslims) and thus supporting and promoting attacks on, and the killing of, non-combatants.

Relevant questions here include the following: (1) Are racism and the promotion of impersonal hatred immoral, bad, harsh? (2) Is the targeting and killing of non-combatants (including women and children) immoral, harsh? According to my criteria - the criteria of my weltanschauung, The Numinous Way - the answer is that they are immoral, bad; they are divisive, impersonal (unempathic), a harsh (an extreme) manifestation of the error, the hubris, that is the-separation-of-otherness. For what is moral is compassion, the peace - the gentleness - of a personal shared love; what is fair, honourable, kind; what manifests the gentility of wu-wei, what manifests the empathic knowing of individuals in the immediacy-of-the-moment.

In the simple sense, all individuals we do not personally know - whom we have not interacted with personally and who thus are unknown to us via, who are inaccessible to, our faculty of empathy - are or should be presumed to be 'innocent', unjudged. Given the benefit of the doubt. For that is the fair, the honourable, the empathic, the humane, thing to do. Thus to promote impersonal goals and objectives - abstractions such as 'suicide attacks' or the hatred and prejudice of racism - which badly affect, harshly impinge upon, which hurt, injure, or kill people we do not know, is assuredly wrong.

My character during my extremist years - or at least the dominant part of my character at the time - was certainly harsh or tended toward being harsh, since my motivation was to harshly pursue, if necessary by violent means, some harsh impersonal goal, some harsh impersonal objective, to engage in activities, with the aim of trying to bring that goal, that objective into-being; with the attainment of that goal, that objective, having immoral priority over virtues such as personal love, personal happiness, compassion, empathy, peace, kindness, and honour. In effect, my life - my deeds, my behaviour, my words (spoken and written) - revealed, proved, that I was indeed an extremist promoting extremism; that I was immoral; that I acted unethically and that I promoted and championed and violently strived for what was wrong.

There is thus in my case - and in the case of others like me - only an acknowledgement of the facts and a recognition of what is moral and what is immoral. For the criteria used are proven deeds, a character directly revealed - individual to individual - by such deeds, and a knowing, an acceptance, by us of what is immoral, bad, wrong.

Race

As mentioned in *FAQ About The Numinous Way* dated 9/March/2012 -

> " Race is a manifestation of the causal separation-of-otherness, and thus contradicts empathy and the intuitive knowing of and sympathy with *the living other* that individual empathy provides or can make us aware of.
>
> The notion of race separates, divides, human beings into manufactured lifeless categories which nullify the empathic knowing of individual human beings. Such assignment of individuals to a posited abstract category - some assumed 'race' or sub-race - is irrelevant, since individual human beings are or have the potential to be unique individual human beings, so that such an assignment, whatever the alleged reason, is a dehumanizing of those individuals. For our humanity is expressed by an individual and personal knowing of individuals, by a personal interaction with others on the basis of respect, tolerance, reason, and honour, and which personal knowledge of them renders their alleged or assumed ethnicity or ancestry irrelevant."

A human being is an individual person who is unique or who has the capacity to be unique, the capacity to develope their uniqueness. Those human beings, those unique individuals, who are not personally known to us, are because they are unknown to us - being thus unseen, unfelt, by our sense, our faculty, of empathy - cannot, should not, be judged by us, or be the subject of or assessed using the assumptions made by us or presented to us by others whether in spoken or in written form. Such is the foundation of The Numinous Way, of the personal weltanschauung I have developed by means of pathei-mathos, where empathy via a direct and extended personal knowing is regarded as the only moral way to really know, to assess, an individual, to discover their physis, their character.

Thus the alleged or assumed 'race' of a person is irrelevant; unimportant. To assume things about someone on the basis of their alleged or assumed 'race' is wrong, contrary to the ethic of empathy and to the honour, the fairness, the compassion, that manifest the knowing that empathy teaches and reveals to us. For 'race' is a supra-personal categorization, an impersonal large-scale grouping, in which the human faculty of empathy, and thus a direct personal knowing of individuals, play no part.

Furthermore, 'race' - however defined - is an abstraction. An ideal and/or a generalization, and a generalization which even taxonomically has no relevance. Thus, even the observed physical, physiological, genetic - the biological - characteristics which have been said to or are alleged to differentiate one human race from another and thus to possibly define separate human races are irrelevant because such differentiation or definitions are by their very nature medians, or assumptions extrapolated from limited data, or an interpretation of data according to a hypothesis, and all of which data are static, time-dependant, relating as they do to a perceived or an assumed commonality existing or alleged to exist 'now' or at some static moment in time but which perceived or assumed commonality did not necessarily exist in the past and will probably, almost certainly, not exist in the future.

For in reality humans change, through social interaction and migration, over millennia so that, for example, some posited so-called 'race' said to exist now in some specific geographic location did not exist twenty thousand years ago (probably not even ten thousand years ago) and the peoples allegedly said to be of this race are and always have been in flux, changing, adapting, assimilating, being assimilated, migrating.

To define such a static 'race' there has to be assumptions made about 'when' it allegedly came into being and about what median values are used to determine if a specific individual 'belongs to' such a race.

But all life - human and otherwise - changes, is subject to change, is in flux. Life changes as it changes [1] and has changed as it has been changed. This is the wisdom of wu-wei; of the physis of things: of beings, of life. To make some posited category the 'ideal' and thus to impute an importance to, and try to preserve, such a static impermanent human-manufactured impersonal 'thing' over and above the flux of life, over and above the wu-wei of individuals, over and above the morality of empathy, compassion, fairness, and over and above the wu-wei of love, is wrong, inhuman, immoral, contrary to the physis of life itself. It is hubris, an ignorance of, or an arrogant disregarding of, The Cosmic Perspective, and thus is a cause of suffering because it upsets the natural balance, the natural harmony, of life.

March 2012

Notes

[1]

ἔστι δ᾽ ὅπη νῦν
ἔστι: τελεῖται δ᾽ ἐς τὸ πεπρωμένον:
οὔθ᾽ ὑποκαίων οὔθ᾽ ὑπολείβων
οὔτε δακρύων ἀπύρων ἱερῶν
ὀργὰς ἀτενεῖς παραθέλξει

Aesch. Ag. 67-71

What is now, came to be
As it came to be. And its ending has been ordained.
No concealed laments, no concealed libations,
No unburnt offering
Can charm away that firm resolve

Acknowledgement: This text summarizes my replies to questions submitted to me in - or which arose during - recent correspondence with several individuals, some of whom raised various objections to my Numinous Way, especially in relation to the concept of 'race' and my use of terms such as 'extremist' and 'extremism'.

Some Notes on The Politics and Ideology of Hate

Part One:
According to the Philosophy of The Numinous Way

Introduction

The ethical criteria of The Numinous Way will be used to consider the politics [1] and the ideology [2] of hate - that is, to consider: (i) those beliefs and/or ideas which produce or which engender or which incite [3] in people an intense dislike of or an extreme or violent aversion to some other people or group and/or of or toward opposing beliefs and/or toward opposing ideas; and (ii) the actions and the political activities of those motivated by or pursuing some ideology that inclines them toward hatred or which produces hatred.

Specific examples will be restricted to two sets of beliefs/ideas, firstly that conventionally termed 'extreme right-wing'/fascist/neo-nazi, and secondly that conventionally termed radical Islam[4], and so restricted for the simple reason that I have personal practical experience of such beliefs/ideas and have also studied them in detail. In the former case, my experience and study amounts to some thirty years; in the latter case, to around nine years.

The Criteria of The Numinous Way

The criteria of The Numinous Way is the revealing - the insight, the knowing, the understanding, the feeling - that the faculty of empathy provides when we, as an individual, personally interact with another living being over a certain period of time. What is thus discovered by means of empathy is *sympatheia* - a numinous sympathy with the-living-other - and how, as an individual, we are an affecting connexion to all life, and thus how our assumed separation, as an individual, is an illusion, a manifestation of hubris. We therefore become aware of how we affect or can affect others; how they affect or can affect us; and of how their suffering, their pain, their joy, their grief, is ours beyond the barrier of our inner and our outer egoist.

This discovery, this revealing, thus inclines us toward compassion, kindness, humility, gentleness, love, tolerance, peace, fairness, wu-wei [5], and toward being non-judgemental in respect of those we do not personally know and thus have no experience of, have had no empathic contact with. For it is empathy - the close and the extended personal interaction with individuals, on an individual basis, that empathy requires - that is the natural and the moral way of assessing, of really knowing, another human being.

This means two important things. First, that we treat human beings in a human way - that is, as individuals, recognizing that they are unique or have the potential to become unique; that they, like us, can and do suffer pain, grief, sadness, joy; that they, like us, have hopes, dreams. Second, that all individuals we do not personally know are or should be presumed to be 'innocent', unjudged, and so are to be given the benefit of the doubt; for this presumption of innocence - until personal experience and empathic individual knowing of them prove otherwise - is the fair, the honourable, the moral thing to do.

The Ideology and Politics of Hate

For an ideology to cause, provoke, or incite hatred - or which inclines people toward hatred or which of itself embodies hate - it is logical to assume that there has to be two components at work given that hatred is an intense personal emotion which can predispose a person or persons toward or cause anger and thence violence, and given that an ideology by its nature is supra-personal, that is, a coherent, organized, and distinctive set of beliefs and/or ideas or ideals.

My experience leads me to suggest that the first component is prideful identity, and that the second component is the ideal, the goal, of the ideology. For this given and accepted identity is always supra-personal and always imparts a needed sense of belonging, a meaning to life, just as the goal, the ideal, involves individuals committing themselves in a manner which vivifies, removes doubt, and imparts a sense of purpose, with the result that individuality becomes subsumed with duty and loyalty to the goal, the ideal, given a high priority in the life of the individual.

Ideologies such as National-Socialism - new or old - and radical Islam are predicated on identity, a pride in that identity, and on the need to affirm that identity through practical deeds. In the case of National-Socialism, there is a personal identification with one's assumed race, a pride in what is believed to be the achievements and the potential of this race, and a desire to aid one's race and its 'destiny' by opposing 'race-mixing'. In the case of radical Islam, there is the sense of belonging to the Ummah, a 'comradeship', a certain pride in Islam and its superiority; a feeling of the need to undertake or at least support Jihad, and a desire to counter the kuffar in practical ways, all deriving from the belief that this is what Allah has commanded we do.

The identity so assumed or presumed produces or can produce resentment, anger - caused by a perceived or a felt disparity between *the now* and *the assumed ideal*, past or future.

For an essential part of such ideologies is that it is believed that in the past some posited ideal community or society or people or way of life existed and that the present is a deviation from or a loss of the 'perfection' that then existed; a deviation or a loss that the ideology explains by the assumption of a simple cause and effect, or several simple causes and effects, a simple linearity between *the now* and *the goal* (future) and/or the idealized past. Thus the problems or the conditions of the present are assumed to have certain identifiable supra-personal causes, just as the path to the goal is regarded as requiring that those causes be dealt with. In addition, these causes are often or mostly the work of 'others'; not our fault, but instead the result of 'our enemies', and/or of some opposing ideology. That is, someone, or some many, or some 'thing', is or are to blame.

Hence in order to return to this past perfection - or in order to create a new form of this past perfection, this past ideal, or in order to create a new perfection inspired by some past ideal - our enemies, and/or opposing ideologies and those adhering to them, must be dealt with. There must therefore be struggle; the notion of future victory; and at the very least political activity and propaganda directed toward political goals - a moving toward regaining the authority, the power, the influence which supporters of an ideology believe or assume they and their kind have lost and which they almost invariably believe are now 'in the hands of their enemies' and/or of traitors and 'heretics'.

In effect, perceived enemies, those having authority/power, and those perceived as adhering to opposing or detrimental ideologies/beliefs or living in a manner seen as detrimental, become dehumanized, are judged en masse in a prejudiced manner, and become disliked, with this dislike naturally - because of the struggle for 'victory' - becoming intolerance, harshness, and thence, almost invariably at some time, turning to anger thence to hatred with such hatred often resulting in violence against individual 'enemies'. [6]

Such hatred and intolerance are the natural, the inevitable, consequence of all ideologies founded on notions of identity which glorify past glories or assumed past perfections, which posit some abstract goal or some future ideal and which involve a struggle against enemies to achieve such a goal or such an ideal.

For there is symbiosis, an empowering of the individual, with the very notion of identity and meaning being dependant on notions about past glories, on inclusion/exclusion, on notions of superiority/inferiority, on posited enemies, on obstacles, and of a striving, a struggle, for an ideal, for some posited goal. And vice versa. This is the intoxicating elixir of extremism, a symbiosis born of, which engenders and which flourishes on division, divide, intolerance, pride, struggle, goals, and hate; a division, divide, an intolerance, a hatred, that possibly are at their worst, their most vitriolic, when based on ethnicity, or involve religions, or involve perceived or assumed 'heretical' divisions within a religion.

In terms of nazi and neo-nazi ideology for example, Aryans are and have been 'the light-bearers of civilization'; the enemies are the Jews and their machinations, inferior non-Aryan races, and ideologies such as 'multi-culturalism' and liberalism; while the goal is a racially pure Aryan nation, and/or a strong and militarized National-Socialist State with a mission, a destiny, to 'civilize' the world through kampf.

In terms of modern right-wing extremism, as manifest for example by certain nationalist political groups in European countries, the 'civilization of the West' - in which many such groups now include Israel [7] - is the ideal because it is morally superior; the enemies (the hated inferiors) are Muslims and other 'immigrants'; with an idealized and resurgent 'European culture and identity' (manifest in strong nation-States of 'native Europeans' and/or in a return to communities based on 'European traditions') having replaced the nazi/fascist ideal of a National-Socialist/Fascist State and with 'past glories' celebrated and idealized and used to motivate and inspire pride and develope a sense of urgency about the 'threat' posed by enemies and by the loss of national/cultural 'identity'.

In terms of radical Islam, the enemies (the hated inferiors) are Amerika, Israel, Muslim collaborators, and decadent kuffar, with the goal being a resurgent Khilafah or at least the implementation of Shariah as the only law at first in

Muslim lands and then elsewhere.

A Numinous Approach

Activists and even many supporters of such ideologies find meaning, worth, identity, empowerment, in the inclusion, in the collectivity, the belonging, that such ideologies assert or assume, and thus their knowing of themselves and of others, and thence their 'ethics' (or lack of ethics) are or become determined by the boundaries set by such ideologies. The boundaries of enemies; of traitors; of those 'different from us/inferior to us'; of obstacles to be overcome in the struggle toward victory; of sacrifice for the cause; of conformity to guidelines for living laid down by a leader or leaders or ideologues or 'the party' or set out in some political programme, or book, or tract, or speech, or manifesto.

What therefore is lost or tends to become lost because of such boundaries, such collectivity, is empathy; wu-wei; notions of the innocence - the non-judgement - of those we do not personally know; *sympatheia* with others on an individual basis; and a desire to treat every human being as an individual sans all ideological boundaries, sans all prejudice, sans abstractions of inclusion/exclusion, sans all notions of 'them' and 'us', and sans all rhetoric and propaganda about a struggle for victory, and about the 'urgency of the situation'.

For such ideologies manifest *the-separation-of-otherness* and which error of hubris is the foundation, the essence, of all abstractions[8], and which *separation-of-otherness* is the genesis of supra-personal, ideological, hatred and intolerance, usurping as such ideologies do with their collective empowerment and their supra-personal authority the empathy of the individual, the unique individual judgement that arises from such empathy, the necessity of interior personal spiritual (numinous) development, and the wu-wei, the compassion, the fairness, the tolerance, the humanity, that empathy by its revealing inclines us toward.

As such, those ideologies, born of and manifesting hubris, ignoring or disrespectful as they are of the numinous, and attempting as they do to redefine the ethical, are therefore - it seems to me - immoral, and lamentable.

2012

Notes

[1] Politics, as used here, means both of the following, according to context. (i) The theory and practice of governance, with governance itself founded on two fundamental assumptions; that of some minority - a government (elected or unelected), some military authority, some oligarchy, some ruling elite, some tyrannos, or some leader - having or assuming authority (and thus power and influence) over others, and with that authority being exercised over a specific

geographic area or territory. (ii) The activities of those individuals or groups whose aim or whose intent is to obtain and exercise some authority or some control over - or to influence - a society or sections of a society by means which are organized and directed toward changing/reforming that society or sections of a society in accordance with a particular ideology.

Ideology, as used here, means a coherent, organized, and distinctive set of beliefs and/or ideas or ideals, and which beliefs and/or ideas and/or ideals pertain to governance, and/or to society, and/or to matters of a philosophical or a spiritual nature.

The term society, as used here, means a collection of people who live in a specific geographic area or areas and whose association or interaction is mostly determined by a shared set of guidelines or principles or beliefs, irrespective of whether these are written or unwritten, and irrespective of whether such guidelines/principles/beliefs are willingly accepted or accepted on the basis of acquiescence.

[2] For the usage, here, of the term ideology see footnote 1.

[3] Incitement is used here in the sense of 'to instigate' or to provoke or to cause or to 'urge others to'.

[4] By radical Islam is meant the belief that practical Jihad against 'the enemies of Islam' and the occupiers of Muslim lands is an individual duty incumbent upon every able-bodied Muslim; that Muslims should live among Muslims under the guidance of Shariah; that Muslims should return to the pure guidance of Quran and Sunnah and distance themselves from the ways and the influence of the kuffar. Many radical Muslims also support the restoration of the Khilafah and are intolerant of those Muslims they consider have allied themselves with the kuffar.

[5] Wu-wei is an important part of The Numinous Way, with the term being used to mean a personal 'letting-be' deriving from a feeling, a knowing, that an essential part of wisdom is cultivation of an interior personal balance and which cultivation requires acceptance that one must work with, or employ, things according to their nature, for to do otherwise is incorrect, and inclines us toward, or is, being excessive – that is, toward the error, the unbalance, that is hubris, an error often manifest in personal arrogance, excessive personal pride, and insolence – that is, a disrespect for the numinous.

In practice, wu-wei is the cultivation of a certain (empathic, numinous) perspective – that life, things/beings, change, flow, exist, in certain natural ways which we human beings cannot change however hard we might try; that such a hardness of human trying, a belief in such hardness, is unwise, un-natural, upsets the natural balance and can cause misfortune/suffering for us and/or for others, now or in the future. Thus success lies in discovering the inner nature (the physis) of things/beings/ourselves and gently, naturally, slowly, working with this inner nature, not striving against it.

[6] One aspect of all extremist ideologies, of the politics and ideologies of hate, that has intrigued me for some time is their explicit or their implicit patriarchal ethos; their masculine bias; their stridency, their lack of not only empathy but also of those qualities that are ineluctably feminine, caring, nurturing, and thus which tend toward balancing the hubriatic male qualities such as harshness, fanaticism, kampf, and militarism, which such ideologies laud.

This bias toward overt masculinity, toward machismo, possibly explains why such harsh, such extremist ideologies - and often the supporters of such ideologies - dislike, are intolerant of, or even hate, pacifists, Sapphic ladies, gay men, and even sensitive artistic men who are not gay.

[7] The support for Israel by such groups has led to some political commentators regarding such support by such extremists as either cynical opportunism or as some attempt to gain political credibility and thus an attempt to distance themselves from nazism and fascism even though their whole agenda, their trumpeting of 'European civilization and culture', their nationalism, their dislike of 'immigrants' and especially of Muslims, seems to place them within the sphere of those ideologies. For instance, these extremists seem to have simply made Muslims, and 'immigrants' in general, the 'new Jews'.

[8] The Numinous Way understands an abstraction as the manufacture, and use of, some idea, ideal, 'image', form, or category, and thus some generalization about, and/or some assignment of an individual or individuals – and/or some being, some 'thing' – to some group or category with the implicit acceptance of the separateness, in causal Space-Time, of such a being/beings/things /individuals. This assignment of human beings to some abstraction (some abstract category) - such as Negro or Jew or 'traitor' or 'heretic' or 'prostitute' - always involves either some pejorative judgement being made about an individual on the basis of the qualities or the attributes that are believed or assumed to belong to that abstraction, or some idealization/glorification of those so assigned (such as some idealized 'Aryan race').

The positing of some 'perfect' or 'ideal' form, category, or thing, is part of abstraction.

Thus understood, abstraction encompasses terms such as ideology, idea, dogmatic/harsh beliefs, and ideals.

°°°

Part Two

A Personal Perspective - My Uncertitude of Knowing

The Bad of Extremists

For some forty years, from 1968 to around 2008, I as a fanatical idealist placed some ideal - some illusory, some believed in perfection - before people, hubristically believing (as fanatics and extremists always seem to do) that some ideology [1] and its attempted implementation was more important than personal love, than fairness, than compassion, than kindness, than tolerance, than empathy, than peace, than wu-wei.

Thus, as a fanatical idealist, I was so dissatisfied, so discontented, with the societies of the West - especially with the society I regarded as my homeland, the United Kingdom - that I actively saught to undermine and change them by political and revolutionary means, by incitement to disaffection and even by terror.

For the first thirty years of this discontent (1968-1998) my desire was to establish, in Britain, a neo-nazi - a racist - society, believing as I did in the superiority of 'the Aryan race' and enamoured as I was of National-Socialist Germany and of Hitler's struggle for power between 1919 and 1933. Thus the idealized, the romanticized, National-Socialism I believed in and the historically-inaccurate NS Germany I admired were my inspiration, and with the dedication and the hardness and harshness of a fanatic, an extremist, I joined several racist, fascist, neo-nazi, and paramilitary organizations; engaged in street brawls, wrote and distributed propaganda, gave vitriolic speeches; organized demonstrations, incited hatred and violence; founded two new neo-nazi groups; was imprisoned for violence and arrested nearly a dozen times for a variety of other criminal offences.

Between 1998 and 2008 - following my conversion to Islam - my activities were directed toward undermining the societies of the West (and especially those of Britain and America) and toward aiding Muslims fighting elsewhere - undertaking Jihad - for the establishment, in their lands, of Shariah as the only law.

During these forty extremist years I ranted and I railed against what I believed were 'the problems of the West', the 'decadence of the West', and propagandistically trumpeted the ideal type of society I believed in and thus considered was better than all existing societies. During my neo-nazi years, this ideal, this idealized, society was a new National-Socialist one, an ideal that I in perhaps some small way helped create through voluminous writings written during the 1990's with titles such as *The Meaning of National-Socialism, Why National-Socialism Is Not Racist*, and *The Complete Guide to the Aryan Way of*

Life. During my Jihadi-supporting years, this ideal, this idealized, society was one inspired by the Khilafah and was to be established in some Muslim land or lands by a return to the pure guidance of Quran and Sunnah, and by Jihad 'against apostates, and the kuffar and their collaborators'.

The error here - the error I persisted in for some forty years - is the error of faulty, unbalanced, judgement, deriving from extremism and hubris; an error that leads to, that develops, that nurtures, bad individuals and thus leads to inhumanity, to violence, prejudice, anger, discontent, hatred, brutality, terrorism. An error caused both by the distorted view of people and of existing societies that extremist ideologies cause or at least encourage, and by some ideal, some ideology, being cherished more than human beings.

For the personal fault of extremists seems to be that of being unable and/or unwilling to view, to consider, the good that exists in people, in society, and/or of ignoring the potential for good, or change toward the good, which is within people, within society, within what-is. To prefer the dream in their head to reality; and/or to prefer the struggle, the strife, the conflict, to stability and peace; and/or to need or to desire repeated stimulation/excitement. One cause of such things could, in my view - from my experience - be the inability or the unwillingness of a person, an extremist, to develope and use their own individual judgement, as well as the inability or the unwillingness to take individual, moral, responsibility for their actions and for the effects those actions personally have upon people. Thus violence, prejudice, hatred, brutality, killing, and terror, are not judged by the moral criteria of how they affect and harm people but instead by whether they aid the goal - the implementation of the cherished ideal - or, worst of all, by whether they provide excitement and/or provide the individual with a sense of purpose, a 'destiny', a sense of being special, a 'hero' to their kindred extremists, or at least of being remembered.

In my own case, I justified what I did - my extremism - by appeals to the goal I ardently believed in and ardently desired, and thus ignored or overlooked or dismissed as unimportant the many benefits that Western societies provide and have provided, concentrating instead on the faults, the problems, of such societies, or on assumed faults and problems. In addition, and most importantly, I arrogantly felt I 'knew', that I 'understood' - that I, or my cherished beliefs, my ideology, were right; correct, *the* solution to all problems, personal and of society, and that these problems urgently needed to be dealt with. There was, therefore, a desire in me to interfere, to act, based on this arrogant misplaced feeling of having 'the right answers', of being right; of having 'seen the flaws' in society and/or in people.

In addition, my judgement derived from, was based on, was dependant upon, The Cause, the ideology; and so was unbalanced, bad, flawed. For The Cause, the ideology, gave meaning and set the boundaries, the limits, of knowing, of doing. For example, in the case of National-Socialism, there was the boundary of duty, which was "to promote National-Socialism [and] to strive to act in

accord with Nature's will by preserving, defending and evolving one's own folk."
[2] There was the meaning of 'pursuing idealism/excellence/the will of Nature' over and above 'personal happiness' as well as the need to 'overthrow the existing System based on materialism' [3]. There was the knowing that 'race and Nature' defined us as human beings so that our most essential knowledge was to know our kind, our 'destiny', and the 'will of Nature', a will manifest, for example, in kampf and idealized in such abstractions as 'a new Reich', Homo Galactica, a Galactic Imperium, and so on and so forth.

The flawed judgement, the lack of critical balance - the lack of humanity - that resulted meant that I did not take individual responsibility for the harm I caused, I inflicted, I incited. Instead, I shifted the responsibility onto the ideology, thus justifying or trying to justify the consequences of my deeds, of my incitement, by appeals to the ideology ('the end justifies the means') and by the belief that the ideology needed to be urgently implemented 'for the good of the people', with 'the people' of course always being viewed abstractly (as a race or folk), being idealized or romanticized and divorced from, or more usually considered as being built from, the harsh consequences of striving to implement such a harsh ideology.

Therefore, it seems to me now that a reasonable illustration of extremism might be to liken it to some contagious disease, some sickness, or some ailment. One that alters not only the behaviour of individuals but also their perception, their thinking; how they perceive the world; and one that inclines them toward being bad and toward ignoring the good that already exists in society and the credit due to society for aiding such good. A disease or an ailment or a sickness that inclines them toward acting in an unbalanced and unethical manner, disruptive to other people and disruptive to society, and careless of, or indifferent to, the harm they do, the suffering they cause.

The Good of Society

The simple truth of the present and so evident to me now - in respect of the societies of the West, and especially of societies such as those currently existing in America and Britain - is that for all their problems and all their flaws they seem to be much better than those elsewhere, and certainly better than what existed in the past. That is, that there is, within them, a certain tolerance; a certain respect for the individual; a certain duty of care; and certainly still a freedom of life, of expression, as well as a standard of living which, for perhaps the majority, is better than elsewhere in the world and most certainly better than existed there and elsewhere in the past.

In addition, there are within their structures - such as their police forces, their governments, their social and governmental institutions - people of good will, of humanity, of fairness, who strive to do what is good, right. Indeed, far more good people in such places than bad people, so that a certain balance, the balance of goodness, is maintained even though occasionally (but not for long) that balance may seem to waver somewhat.

Furthermore, many or most of the flaws, the problems, within such societies are recognized and openly discussed, with a multitude of people of good will, of humanity, of fairness, dedicating themselves to helping those affected by such flaws, such problems. In addition, there are many others trying to improve those societies, and to trying find or implement solutions to such problems, in tolerant ways which do not cause conflict or involve the harshness, the violence, the hatred, of extremism. [4]

This truth about the good [5] in our current societies, so evident now, leads me to ask how could I not have seen it before? How can extremists, in general, not see, understand, appreciate, this truth? How can they - as I once did - seek to destroy that balance; destroy all that such societies, despite their flaws and their problems, have achieved? How can they ignore the good work of the plethora of individuals seeking to change those societies for the better in a reasoned and tolerant manner?

I can only, in truth, answer for myself, based on some years of introspection. As an extremist in thrall to an ideology and thus seeking to disrupt, change, to overthrow an existing society - to incite disaffection - I had no reason, no incentive, to emphasize the good that had and has been wrought by successive governments, by the introduction of laws, and by the people, such as the police and the security services, who in their majority tried from the best of motives to do and to uphold what was good by striving to counter and bring to justice those who who were bad, those who in some way harmed or saught to harm others from whatever motive and for whatever reason.

Indeed, I was for the most part wilfully ignorant of this good, and when mention or experience of it could not be ignored for some reason, or might prove useful for propaganda purposes, what was good was almost always attributed to something which the parameters of the ideology allowed for. For instance, the good actions of an heroic policeman would be judged by the parameters of whether he was 'Aryan' - in which case 'the good' resulted from him being Aryan, having an Aryan nature - or whether those actions in some way, however small, helped 'us' and our Cause, as for example if the person in question had dealt with and caught 'black people' rioting or committing crimes. There was thus a biased, a blinkered, a prejudiced, a bigoted view of both events and people.

In my own case, and for example, I have some forty years experience of interaction with the police, from ordinary constables and detectives, to custody sergeants, to officers from specialist branches such as SO12, SO13, and crime squads. During that time, I have known far more good police officers than bad - corrupt - ones. Furthermore, I realized that most of those I came into contact with were good individuals, motivated by the best of intentions, who were trying to do their best, often under difficult circumstances, and often to help victims of dishonourable deeds, catch those responsible for such deeds, and/or prevent such deeds.

But what did I during my extremist years attribute their honourable motivation, their good character, to? Yes, of course - to them being 'Aryans' who just happened to be in the police force. Or, on one occasion, to having an 'Aryan nature' (accorded honorary Aryan status) even though the officer in question was 'of mixed race'... Thus the ideology I adhered to, I believed in, set the parameters of my judgement; prompted the correct ideological response [6].

But in truth they, those officers, as one of them once said to me, were guided by what 'was laid down' and did not presume to or tried hard not to overstep their authority; guided as they were by the law, that accumulated received wisdom of what was and is good in society; a law which (at least in Britain and so far as I know) saught to embody a respect for what was fair and which concept of fairness was and always has been (again, at least in Britain and so far as I know) untainted, uncorrupted, by any political ideology.

Now I know, I understand, I appreciate, that for that reason - of so being mindful of the limits of their authority, of being guided by what had been laid down over decades - those people, those police officers, were far better individuals than the arrogant, the hubriatic, extremist I was; an arrogant extremist who by and for himself presumed 'to know' what was right, who presumed to understand, who presumed he possessed the ability, the authority, and the right to judge everyone and everything, and who because of such arrogance, such hubris, most certainly continued to contribute to the cycle of suffering, ignoring thus for so long as he in his unbalance did the wisdom that Aeschylus gave to us in *The Oresteia*.

Balance and The Uncertitude of Knowing

One error of unbalance and of hubris - and an error which is one of the foundations of extremism - is that of allowing or of encouraging some imagined, idealized, or posited, future to affect one's judgement, and/or to determine one's actions, and behaviour in the present.

Thus one becomes not only dissatisfied with what-is, but concerned with - if not to some extent obsessed with - what *should-be* or what *might-be* if what should-be (the goal or ideal of the extremist ideology) is not realized or not fought for. Furthermore, this assumed *what-might-be* is often the result of someone making some generalization or some prediction based on some ideology and which ideology, being an ideology - an abstraction - is founded on the simplicity of linear cause-and-effect and of problems/enemies having to be dealt with in order for some perfect future or some ideal or some victory to be achieved or brought-into-being. That is, *what-might-be* - and extremist action and incitement based upon it - requires a certainty of knowing.

This is one error I persisted in even after - as a result of pathei-mathos - I began to fully develope my philosophy of The Numinous Way with its emphasis on empathy, compassion, humility, and personal honour. An error which, for example, led to me, for some two or more years, to ebucinate the abstraction of 'the clan' as some sort of embodiment of 'the numinous' and of honour and as an idealized means of manufacturing a new type of society as if such a future, such an assumed, hypothesized, society might offset some of the suffering in the world.

An error which the uncertitude of empathic knowing most certainly reveals. For empathy - the living, the numinous, way to know another living being - is a sympatheia, sans all ideations, with a living being in the immediacy-of-the-moment and involves an individualized proximity, and thus discovers only the knowing of that one living being as that living being is in that one moment, or those moments, of empathy. A discovery applicable to only that specific being and a knowing which some future empathic discovery in respect of that same being might change. For living beings are subject to change; their life is a flow, possessed of an a-causal living nature; and thus another encounter with that same living being may reveal it changed, altered - perhaps better, or matured - in some manner. Certainly, in respect of human beings, pathei-mathos is or can be a vector of interior change.

Thus, the faculty of empathy - over a succession of moments linked in causal time by a duration of days, weeks, or months - may intimate to us something about the character, the nature, the physis, of another person. A subsequent meeting with that individual - months, years, later - may intimate a change in that nature, possibly as a result of pathei-mathos.

There thus arises the knowing of the wu-wei, the humanity, of empathy; a knowing of the transient, the a-causal, nature of the living-knowing, the revealing, the a-causal knowledge, that empathy may provide, and hence the need not to judge, not to prejudge, some past or future living being (or even the same being once known) unknown to, or as yet untouched by, such empathy or by another empathic encounter. For certitude of knowing - presumed, assumed, or otherwise - is causal, fixed, or the result of some posited linear extrapolation of such a static causal knowing into the future or back into some past.

Extremism - of whatever type - depends on this certitude of knowing, past and future, and which certitude amounts to a tyranny against the flow of life; certainly there is a lack of empathy, as well as the imposition of and thence the cultivation of a rigid harshness within the psyche of the individual which at best displaces, or which can displace, the human capacity for pathei-mathos, and which at worst may remove the capacity for pathei-mathos.

The future certitude of this hubriatic knowing is the given and fixed goal or ideal; and the certitude of struggle being necessary to reach that future goal or make real that ideal. The past certitude is of a given idealized past and/or of past glories (if indeed they were glories). And the present certitude is that of identity - of 'we' being different from and better than 'them'. A certitude of identity and of assumed difference that gives rise to prejudice, hatred, intolerance, and all the other characteristics of the extremist.

Thus, for a neo-nazi or a racist, 'Aryans' (or 'Whites') are regarded as superior to 'blacks' and Jews, and the 'separation of the races' is regarded as the ideal goal. This superiority is a given, an affirmed, certitude, and regarded as fixed, past, present, future, and applicable to most if not all of the 'inferior' group or groups. There is thus no uncertitude of knowing in the individual; no interior balance; no wu-wei; no empathic discovery of the character, the nature, the physis, of other individuals as individuals in the immediacy-of-the moment; no allowance made for change, even by pathei-mathos. There is only harshness; generalization, supposition, assumption; a rigid adherence; the arrogance of certainty, of 'knowing' some are superior/inferior, that there is black/white, Aryan/Jew; that separation is 'necessary' and desirable. A need for stasis, and/or the desire to inhumanly try to make living, changing, individual, human beings fit some static category and thence the prejudice and intolerance and hatred based on or resulting from such an assumed or idealized static category.

As I know from my own experience, the certitude of knowing and the certitude of identity that an ideology provides displaces personal love, fairness, compassion, kindness, tolerance, empathy, peace, and wu-wei; or at least assigns to them a far lower importance than hate, injustice, harshness, intolerance, prejudice, strife, and disaffection to society, to what-is. Such certitude, such a lack of the humanity of empathy, also provides us with a fixed, an - according to my pathei-mathos, my experience - incorrect, answer to an important question attributed to Aeschylus and asked over two thousand years ago, and which fixed incorrect answer encourages, breeds, plants, the τύραννος within us [7] - our hubris, our inner egoist - and which wrong answer encourages, which breeds, which plants, tyrannical societies as well as allowing such a τύραννος as Hitler to gain an abundance of followers obedient to his hubriatic will.

The important question is τίς οὖν ἀνάγκης ἐστὶν οἰακοστρόφος [8]. And the fixed and the incorrect answer is always the same: some leader, some τύραννος, some sovereign, some ideology, some goal, some rigid identity, is there to guide us, to provide us with meaning, to justify our actions. To explain away or justify our lack of empathy, our lack of compassion, our intolerance, our suspicion, our hatred; our lack of wu-wei; and our lack of respect of the numinous, our lack of respect for other life, for human beings different from us. A wrong answer to explain our amnesia, our forgetting or ignorance of the wisdom of the past; a wisdom embodied in what - at least according to my admittedly fallible judgement, born from my pathei-mathos - is the correct answer given to that question asked thousands of years ago and which correct answer is in my view an excellent reply to extremism. An answer which embodies that uncertitude of knowing that is the essence of balance and which uncertitude the faculty of empathy makes us aware of. For the answer to preventing the extremism of hubris, to who guides us, who steers us, to whom we should look, and whom respect, is: Μοῖραι τρίμορφοι μνήμονές τ᾽ Ἐρινύες [9].

April 2012

Notes

[1] I have outlined, in part one, what I mean by terms such as ideology, society, politics, and wu-wei. As explained in several other essays - such as *Ethos of Extremism* - by extreme I mean *to be harsh*, so that an *extremist* is a person who tends toward harshness, or who is harsh, or who supports/incites harshness, in pursuit of some objective, usually of a political or a religious nature; where *harsh* is understood as rough, severe, a tendency to be unfeeling, unempathic.

[2] *The Meaning of National-Socialism* (dated 108yf, i.e. 1997)

[3] *ibid*.

[4] In my essay *Society, Social Reform, and The Numinous Way* (dated February 2012) I briefly touched upon 'a numinous approach' to social change and reform. Which was the apolitical, non-violent one of personal example, and of fostering, encouraging, the natural, slow, interior and personal change of individuals.

[5] The good is what is fair; what alleviates or does not cause suffering; what is compassionate; what empathy by its revealing inclines us to do.

[6] It was such experiences - personal and political - which eventually, after two and half decades, prompted me in the late 1990's to modify my ideology and thus develope what I termed non-racist 'ethical National-Socialism'. But even that did not alter my commitment to extremism, my extremist activities, and my desire to undermine and overthrow British society.

[7] ὕβρις φυτεύει τύραννον. 'Hubris plants the tyrant.' Sophocles: *Oedipus Tyrannus*, v. 872.

[8] "Who then compels to steer us?" *Aeschylus* [attributed], *Prometheus Bound*, 515

[9] "Trimorphed Moirai with their ever-heedful Furies!" *Aeschylus* [attributed], *Prometheus Bound*, 516.

Some Philosophical and Moral Problems of National-Socialism

Introduction

This essay is a brief analysis of the National-Socialist weltanschauung, as manifested in National-Socialist Germany, and according to the philosophical and ethical criteria of my Numinous Way, and which criteria derive from the principles of empathy, compassion, and personal honour.

Empathy, as understood by my philosophy of The Numen [1], establishes a particular ontology and epistemology; Being, the source of beings, as both causal and acausal, and of an acausal knowing distinct from the causal knowing of conventional philosophy and empirical science [2]. The ethical criteria are manifest in both compassion and honour [3], so that:

> "the morality of The Numinous Way is therefore defined by a personal honour, a personal compassion, and the personal virtue of justice. For justice is not some abstract concept, but rather a personal virtue, as εὐταξία is a personal virtue. For justice is the personal virtue of fairness; the quality of balance." *War and Violence in the Philosophy of The Numinous Way*

The National-Socialism evident in NS Germany was a way of life centred around concepts such as duty, *kampf*, nation, and race. Thus, the individual was judged by, and expected to judge others by, the criteria of race, with particular races assigned a certain value (high or low), as individuals were judged by how well they adhered to the duty they were expected to do in respect of their nation (their land, their people) and the race they were said to belong to or believed they belonged to. In addition, *kampf* between individuals, races, and nations was considered healthy and necessary, with such struggle revealing the worth of individuals and thus those considered fit to lead and assume positions of authority.

Collectivism, Nationalism, and Race

The National-Socialist way of life was – given such concepts as *kampf*, nation and race – a collective one, with one of the highest virtues being the willingness of individuals, if necessary, to sacrifice their own happiness and welfare, and even their lives, for the good of their people, their land, their race. The necessity of this virtue was explained, in part, by the belief that the German *volk* had an historic mission, a particular destiny, so that – coupled with the ideas of race and *kampf* - the individual was expected to define themselves, to understand themselves, as Germans and as having particular duties and obligations; in effect, to replace their own self-identity with the collective identity of the volk.

In order to establish, maintain, and expand this collectivism, certain measures were regarded as necessary, as morally correct, with such measures including military conscription, laws designed to criminalize certain activities, both political and personal, and harsh punishment of those contravening such laws.

In addition, the *führerprinzip* was applied to most aspects of life, with individuals expected to accept and obey the authority so established, since such authority was considered to manifest the will, the ethos, of the *volk*. Hence the loyalty individuals gave, as an expression of their recognized duty as Germans, was personal; not to 'the State' nor even to 'the nation', and certainly not to some government, but rather to individuals who were regarded as embodying the will, the identity, of the volk. In practice, this meant Adolf Hitler and those appointed by him or by his representatives, and it was this collectivism, this binding of the *volk* by the *führerprinzip*, that Heidegger tried to philosophically express in his now controversial remarks regarding the *Volksgemeinschaft* and by quoting some words attributed to Aeschylus [4].

There are thus six elements that, from the philosophical and ethical viewpoint of The Numinous Way, may be said to define the National-Socialism of Adolf Hitler. These are: (i) a collective identity and its acceptance; (ii) authority and its acceptance manifest in specific individuals and expected obedience to such authority; (iii) mandatory enforceable punishment of those contravening or not accepting such authority and the laws made by such authority; (iv) the use of particular abstractions (for example nation and race) as a criteria for judgement and for evaluating individual worth; (v) the use of particular abstractions as a criteria for identity; and (vi) the use and acceptance of a particular abstraction – *kampf* – as an embodiment and expression of human nature.

Contra The National-Socialism of Adolf Hitler

In purely practical terms, the acceptance and use of the principle of kampf together with the acceptance of Hitler as embodying the collective will of the *volk*, inevitably led to the military defeat of NS Germany. For all mortals are fallible and military defeat is always inevitable, given time and even if such a defeat has internal, not external, causes. For tyrants and monarchs die, are overthrown, or are killed; Empires flourish for a while – a few centuries perhaps, at most – and then invariably decline and fade away; oligarchies come and go with monotonous regularity, lasting a decade or perhaps somewhat longer; rebellions and revolutions will break out, given sufficient time, and will often succeed given even more time – decades, centuries – and even following repeated and brutal repression.

Thus, philosophically, the general error here by Hitler and his followers was the obvious one of ὕβρις. A lack of understanding, an unknowing, of the natural balance – of δίκη - as well as a lack of empathy, manifest as this unknowing, this lack, was in the arrogant belief of a personal and a volkish 'destiny' combined with a belief in *kampf* as a natural and necessary expression of human nature. And ὕβρις φυτεύει τύραννον - that is, ὕβρις plants, is the seed of, the τύραννον. Thus, symbolically, we might justifiably say that the Ἐρινύες took their revenge, for Hitler and his followers had forgotten, scorned, or never known the wisdom, the truth, that their fallible mortal lives are subject to, guided by, Μοῖραι τρίμορφοι μνήμονές τ' Ἐρινύες [5]. Thus their fate was destined, a fate that Sophocles expressed so well in respect of Oedipus, *tyrannus*:

ὦ πάτρας Θήβης ἔνοικοι, λεύσσετ', Οἰδίπους ὅδε,
ὃς τὰ κλείν' αἰνίγματ' ᾔδει καὶ κράτιστος ἦν ἀνήρ,
οὗ τίς οὐ ζήλῳ πολιτῶν ἦν τύχαις ἐπιβλέπων,
εἰς ὅσον κλύδωνα δεινῆς συμφορᾶς ἐλήλυθεν.
ὥστε θνητὸν ὄντα κείνην τὴν τελευταίαν ἰδεῖν
ἡμέραν ἐπισκοποῦντα μηδέν' ὀλβίζειν, πρὶν ἂν
τέρμα τοῦ βίου περάσῃ μηδὲν ἀλγεινὸν παθών. [6]

In effect, therefore, and in general terms, the National-Socialism of Adolf Hitler was un-wise; based on a mis-understanding of human nature, and he himself shown, despite his remarkable achievement of gaining power, as lacking a reasoned, a well-balanced, judgement [σωφρονεῖν] – since such a balanced judgement would, as Aeschylus explained in the *Oresteia*, reveal that πόλεμος [7] always accompanies ὕβρις and that only by acceptance of the numinous authority of πάθει μάθος (the new law presented to mortals by immortal Zeus) could the tragic cycle of ἔρις be ended.

A Numinous View of The National-Socialism of Adolf Hitler

Let us now consider the six points enumerated above, in respect of the philosophical and ethical viewpoint of The Numinous Way.

As mentioned in my essay *A Brief Numinous View of Religion, Politics, and The State:*

"The essence of the numinous view – of the ethical way posited by the Philosophy of The Numen – is empathy and thus the acausal (the affective and effecting) connexion we, as individuals, are to all life, sentient and otherwise, with empathy being the foundation of our conscious humanity.

The practical criteria which empathy implies is essentially two-fold: the criteria of the cessation of suffering, and the criteria of the individual, personal, judgement in the immediacy of the moment. For the Philosophy of The Numen, these two criteria manifest the natural character of rational, conscious, empathic, human beings and thus express the nature of our humanity and of human culture, and which nature is manifest in a practical way in compassion and in personal honour.

Hence these two criteria are used, by The Numinous Way – by the Philosophy of The Numen – to judge our actions, our personal behaviour, and also all the abstractions we manufacture or may manufacture and which thus affect us, as individuals."

(i) A collective identity and its acceptance.

Empathy, as a natural if still under-used and under-developed human faculty, is only and ever individual and of the immediacy of the living moment. [8] It is always personal, individual, and cannot cannot be abstracted out from an individual living being – that is, it cannot have any causal ideation or be represented by or expressed by someone else.

There is the personal, individual, freedom that the knowing that empathy uniquely presents to the individual, and therefore no need of, no sense of, belonging to other than one's immediate surroundings, and no sense of identity beyond the personally known, for all human beings encountered are encountered and empathically known as they uniquely are: as individuals with their own lives, feelings, hopes, and with their own potential and their own past.

Which in essence means The Numinous Way is the way of individuals, and an individual manner of living to be accepted or rejected according to the individual. Thus such a collective identity – and a desire for and acceptance of such an identity – is contrary to this very individual numinous way.

What matters for The Numinous Way is the individual; their empathy, their honour; their personal judgement. What does not matter are supra-personal manufactured abstractions such as a 'nation'. Consequently, the empathic, honourable, individual only has a duty to themselves, to their immediate kin, and to those personally given a pledge of loyalty: not a duty or obligations to some manufactured collective identity however such identity be expressed.

(ii) Authority and its acceptance manifest in specific individuals and expected obedience to such authority.

As I wrote in *Authority and Legitimacy in the Philosophy of The Numinous Way*:

" For The Numinous Way, it is the exercise of the judgement of the individual – arising from the use of empathy and the guidance that is personal honour – that is paramount, and which expresses our human nature.

That is, it is honour, the understanding that empathy provides, and the judgement of the individual, that are legitimate, moral, numinous, and thence the basis for authority. This means that authority resides in and extends only to individuals – by virtue of their honour, their empathy, and manifest in their own personal judgement, and therefore this always personal individual authority cannot be abstracted out from such personal judgement of individuals. In practical terms, this is a new type of authority – that of the individual whose concern is not power over others but over themselves, and which type of power is manifest in a living by honour, and thence in their self-responsibility and in how they interact with others."

Thus, such non-individual authority, acceptance of and obedience to such authority, is contrary to The Numinous Way.

(iii) Mandatory enforceable punishment of those contravening or not accepting such authority and the laws made by such authority.

Given that, for The Numinous Way, authority and justice are individual and manifest in individual judgement and through personal honour, such mandatory punishment by some abstract authority is quite contrary to The Numinous Way.

(iv) The use of particular abstractions (for example nation and race) as a criteria for judgement and for evaluating individual worth.

According to both empathy and honour, such a judgement of others, such prejudice, on the basis of some abstraction such as perceived race or 'nationality' is immoral [9]. The only moral, honourable, criteria is to judge *individuals* as individuals, sans all abstractions, on the basis of a personal knowing of them extending over a duration of causal Time. To judge *en masse*, without such a direct, personal, extended, personal knowing of each and every individual is reprehensible.

In addition, it is immoral – unempathic, uncompassionate, dishonourable – to treat people on the basis of their assumed or alleged race or nationality. Thus, the enforced herding of people into 'concentration camps' on the basis of alleged, assumed, race or nationality is quite unjustifiable, inhuman.

(v) The use of particular abstractions as a criteria for identity.

Such abstractions included 'blood' and nationality, so that identity became a matter of individuals being classified – by themselves, others, and by the State – according to certain chosen abstract criteria based on 'race' and heritage. Thus there were distinct notions, distinct levels, of separateness.

Empathy, however, presents us with an acausal-knowing of life, human and otherwise, and this knowing is of ourselves as but one fallible, biologically fragile, mortal, microcosmic nexion, and thus of how our self, our perceived and singular separate self-identity, is appearance and not an expression of the true nature of our being [10], which nature is one of connexions, between living emanations, not one of separations.

Such a revealing of our nature reveals that we should act with empathy and honour in the knowledge that our actions affect others or can affect others, directly, indirectly, emotionally, and acausally. That their joy, their pain, their suffering, their fate is ours by virtue of us as a connexion to them – as a connexion to all life; as one emanation of ψυχή [11].

What abstractions do is that they conceal our true empathic, compassionate, honourable nature and, ultimately, sever the connexion we are to ψυχή, to The Numen.

As mentioned in *On The Nature of Abstractions:*

> " The error of abstractionism – of using existing abstractions and manufacturing other abstractions and using these as the source of ethics, of judgement, and so ascribing a value to them – is the error of ὕβρις (hubris). That is, the error of unbalance: of neglecting or being unaware of empathy, and of neglecting or being unaware of or profaning the numinous. In the personal and social sense, ὕβρις is revealed in a lack of compassion, a lack of balanced reasoning, and not only ascribing to one's self (or some other abstraction, such as a nation-State) what is assumed to be the perfection of right and of good (or the best current approximation of it) but also acting on that presumption to the detriment, the harm, of others.
>
> This is unethical – as all abstractions are inherently unethical – because what is ethical is determined by empathy, and thus cannot be abstracted out of that direct, immediate, and personal knowing which presences empathy in us, as human beings."

(vi) The use and acceptance of a particular abstraction – *kampf* – as an embodiment and expression of human nature.

As mentioned previously, in the *Contra The National-Socialism of Adolf Hitler* section, *kampf* as principle, as abstraction, is a manifestation of the error of ὕβρις and of a lack of empathy.

For empathy, and the cultivation of σωφρονεῖν, incline us toward – or should incline us, as individuals, toward – a letting-be; to wu-wei; to a living in the immediacy-of-the-moment. To being compassionate and honourable human beings, concerned only with our own affairs, that of our family, and that of our immediate locality where we dwell, work, and have-our-being.

In addition:

> "In The Numinous Way, a distinction is made between war and *combat* in that combat refers to *gewin* – similar to the old Germanic *werra*, as distinct from the modern *krieg*. That is, combat refers to a more personal armed quarrel between much smaller factions (and often

between just two adversaries – as in single combat, and trial by combat) when there is, among those fighting, some personal matter at stake or some personal interest involved, with most if not all of those fighting doing so under the leadership of someone they personally know and respect and with the quarrel usually occurring in the locality or localities where the combatants live.

Thus, war is contrary to The Numinous Way – to the Cosmic Ethic – not only because of the impersonal suffering it causes, but also because it is inseparably bound up with individuals having to relinquish their own judgement, with them pursuing some lifeless un-numinous abstraction by violent means, and with the development of supra-personal abstract and thus un-numinous notions of 'justice' and law.

Hence, there is, for The Numinous Way, no such thing as a 'just war' – for war is inherently unjust and un-numinous. What is just and lawful are honourable individuals and their actions, and such combat as such individuals may honourably and personally undertake, and such violence as they may honourably and of necessity employ in pursuit of being fair and ensuring fairness." *War and Violence in the Philosophy of The Numinous Way*

Conclusion

It should thus be quite clear why The Numinous Way is contrary to and incompatible with the National-Socialism of Adolf Hitler that was manifest in National-Socialist Germany.

January 2012
Revised JD2455956.107

————————

Notes

[1] Refer, for example, to *Introduction to The Philosophy of The Numen* and also *The Natural Balance of Honour – Honour, Empathy, and Compassion in the Philosophy of The Numinous Way*, from which this is a quote:

> "As used and defined by The Numinous Way, empathy – ἐμπάθεια – is a natural human faculty: that is, a noble intuition about another human being or another living being. When empathy is developed and used, as envisaged by The Numinous Way, it is a specific and extended type of συμπάθεια. That is, it is a type of and a means to knowing and understanding another human being and/or other living beings – and thus differs in nature from compassion."

[2] See: (i) *An Introduction To The Ontology of Being*; (ii) *Some Notes Concerning Causality, Ethics, and Acausal Knowing*; (iii) *Acausality, Phainómenon, and The Appearance of Causality*.

[3] qv. *The Natural Balance of Honour*.

[4] In his 1933 speech at the University of Freiburg, where he quoted the following verse (v.514) from *Prometheus Bound* [my translation] –

> τέχνη δ᾿ ἀνάγκης ἀσθενεστέρα μακρῷ.

> How so very feeble Craft is before Compulsion!

[5]

> τίς οὖν ἀνάγκης ἐστὶν οἰακοστρόφος.
> Μοῖραι τρίμορφοι μνήμονές τ᾿ Ἐρινύες

> Who then compels to steer us?
> Trimorphed Moirai with their ever-heedful Furies!

> *Aeschylus* (attributed), *Prometheus Bound*, 515-6 [My translation]

[6]

> You natives of Thebes: Observe – here is Oedipus,
> He who understood that famous enigma and was a strong man:
> What clansman did not behold that fortune without envy?
> But what a tide of problems have come over him!
> Therefore, look toward that ending which is for us mortals,
> To observe that particular day – calling no one lucky until,
> Without the pain of injury, they are conveyed beyond life's ending.

> *Oedipus Tyrannus, vv. 1524-1530 [My translation]*

[7] In respect of πόλεμος see my *The Abstraction of Change as Opposites and Dialectic* where I suggest that as used by Heraclitus it implies neither kampf nor conflict, but rather – as a quote from Diogenes Laërtius suggests – what lies behind or beyond Phainómenon; that is, non-temporal, non-causal, Being. πόλεμος is thus that which is or becomes the genesis of beings from Being, and also that which manifests as δίκη and accompanies ἔρις because it is the nature of Πόλεμος that beings, born because of and by ἔρις, can be returned to Being (become bound together – be whole – again) by enantiodromia.

[8] Refer, for example, to *Introduction to The Philosophy of The Numen*

[9] See *Empathy and The Immoral Abstraction of Race* and also *On The Nature of Abstractions*.

[10] Refer for example to *Acausality, Phainómenon, and The Appearance of Causality* and also *An Introduction To The Ontology of Being*.

[11] Correctly understood – and as evident by the usage of Homer, Aeschylus, Aristotle, et al – ψυχή implies Life *qua* being.

Suffering And The Human Culture Of Pathei-Mathos
Extract From A Letter To A Personal Correspondent

In respect of the question whether I am optimistic about our future as a species, I vacillate between optimism and pessimism, knowing as I – and so many – do from experience that the world contains people who do good things [1], people who do bad things, and people who when influenced or led or swayed by some-thing or someone can veer either way; and given that it seems as if in each generation there are those – many – who have not learned or who cannot learn from the pathei-mathos of previous generations, from our collective human πάθει μάθος that has brought-into-being a culture of pathei-mathos thousands of years old. Historically – prior to, during, after the time of Cicero, and over a thousand years later during and after the European Renaissance – this culture was evident in Studia Humanitatis, and is now presenced in works inspired by or recollecting personal pathei-mathos and described in memoirs, aural stories, and historical accounts; in particular works of literature, poetry, and drama; in non-verbal mediums such as music and Art, and by art-forms such as films and documentaries.

This culture of pathei-mathos reveals to us the beauty, the numinosity, of personal love; the numinosity of humility, and compassion; and the tragic lamentable unnecessary suffering caused by hubris, dishonour, selfishness, inconsiderance, intolerance, prejudice, hatred, war, extremism, and ideologies [2]. A world-wide suffering so evident, today, for example in the treatment of and the violence (by men) toward women; in the continuing armed conflicts – regional and local, over some-thing – that displace tens of thousands of people and cause destruction, injury, and hundreds of thousands of deaths; and evident also in the killing of innocent people [3] by those who adhere to a harsh interpretation of some religion or some political ideology.

Do good people, world-wide, outweigh bad ones? My experiences and travels incline me to believe they may do, although it seems as if the damage the bad ones do, the suffering they cause, sometimes and for a while outweighs the good that others do. But does the good done, in societies world-wide, now outweigh the bad done, especially such large-scale suffering as is caused by despots, corruption, armed conflict, and repressive regimes? Probably, at least in some societies. And yet even in such societies where, for example, education is widespread, there always seem to be selfish, dishonourable, inconsiderate, people; and also people such as the extremist I was with my hubriatic certitude-of-knowing inciting or causing hatred and violence and intolerance and glorifying war and kampf and trying to justify killing in the name of some abstraction or some belief or some cause or some ideology. People mostly, it seems, immune to and/or intolerant of the learning of the culture of pathei-mathos; a learning available to us in literature, music, Art, memoirs, in the aural and written recollections of those who endured or who witnessed hatred, violence, intolerance, conflict, war, and killing, and a learning also available in the spiritual message of those who taught humility, goodness, love, and tolerance. Immune or intolerant people who apparently can only change – or who could only possibly change for the better – only when they themselves are afflicted by such vicissitudes, such personal misfortune and suffering, as is the genesis of their own pathei-mathos.

Thus, and for example, in Europe there is the specific pathei-mathos that the First and the Second World Wars wrought. A collective learning regarding the destruction, the suffering, the brutality, the horror, of wars where wrakeful machines and mass manufactured weapons played a significant role.

All this, while sad, is perhaps the result of our basic human nature; for we are jumelle, and not only because we are "deathful of body yet deathless the inner mortal" [4] but also because it seems to me that what is good and bad resides in us all [5], nascent or alive or as part of our personal past, and that it is just so easy, so tempting, so enjoyable, sometimes, to indulge in, to do, what is bad, and often harder for us to do what is right. Furthermore, we do seem to have a tendency – or perhaps a need – to ascribe what is bad to being 'out there', in something abstract or in others while neglecting or not perceiving our own faults and mistakes and while asserting or believing that we, and those similar to us or who we are in agreement with, are right and thus have the 'correct', the righteous, answers. Thus it is often easier to find what is bad 'out there' rather than within ourselves; easier to hate than to love, especially as a hatred of impersonal others sometimes affords us a reassuring sense of identity and a sense of being 'better' than those others.

Will it therefore require another thousand, or two thousand, or three thousand years – or more or less millennia – before we human beings en masse, world-wide, are empathic, tolerant, kind, and honourable? Is such a basic change in our nature even possible? Certainly there are some – and not only ideologues of one kind or another – who would argue and who have argued that such a change is not desirable. And is such a change in our nature contingent, as I incline to believe, upon the fair allocation of world resources and solving problems such as hunger and poverty and preventing preventable diseases? Furthermore, how can or could or should such a basic change be brought about – through an organized religion or religions, or through individual governments and their laws and their social and political and economic and educational policies, or through a collocation of governments, world-wide; or through individuals reforming themselves and personally educating others by means of, for example, the common culture of pathei-mathos which all humans share and which all human societies have contributed to for thousands of years?

Which leads us on to questions regarding dogma, faith, and dissent; and to questions regarding government and compulsion and 'crime and punishment' and whether or not 'the needs of the many outweigh the needs of the few'; and also to questions regarding the efficacy of the reforming, spiritual, personal way given that spiritual ways teaching love, tolerance, humility, and compassion – and virtuous as they are, and alleviating and preventing suffering as they surely have – have not after several thousand years effected such a change in humans en masse.

I have to admit that I have no definitive or satisfactory answers to all these, and similar, questions; although my own pathei-mathos – and my lamentable four-decade long experience as an extremist, an ideologue, and as a selfish opinionated inconsiderate person – incline me to prefer the reforming, spiritual, personal way since I feel that such an approach, involving as it does a personal study of, a personal transmission of, the culture of pathei-mathos – and a personal knowing and a living of the humility that the culture of pathei-mathos teaches – is a way that does not cause nor contribute to the suffering that still so blights this world. A personal preference for such a numinous way even though I am aware of three things: of my past propensity to be wrong and thus of the necessary fallible nature of my answers; of the limited nature and thus the long time-scale (of many millennia) that such a way implies; and that it is possible, albeit improbable except in Science Fiction, that good people of honourable intentions may some day find a non-suffering-causing way by which governments or society or perhaps some new form of governance may in some manner bring about that change, en masse, in our human nature required to evolve us into individuals of empathy, compassion, and honour, who thus have something akin to a 'prime directive' to guide them in their dealings with those who are different, in whatever way, from ourselves.

Were I to daydream about some future time when such a galactic 'prime directive' exists, directing we spacefaring humans not to interfere in the internal affairs of non-terrans who are different, in whatever way, from ourselves, then I would be inclined to speculate that unless we by then have fundamentally and irretrievably changed ourselves for the better then it would not be long before some human or some human authority, somewhere, manufactured some sly excuse to order to try and justify ignoring it. For that is what we have done, among ourselves, for thousands of years; making then breaking some treaty or other; making some excuse to plunder resources; having some legal institution change some existing law or make some new law to give us the 'right' to do what it is we want to do; or manufacture some new legislative or governing body in order to 'legalize' what we do or have already done. Always using a plethora of words – and, latterly, legalese – to persuade others, and often ourselves, that what we do or are about to do or have already done is justified, justifiable, necessary, or right.

Perhaps the future excuse to so interfere contrary to a prime directive would be the familiar one of 'our security'; perhaps it would be an economic one of needing to exploit 'their' resources; perhaps it would be one regarding the threat of 'terrorism'; perhaps it would be the ancient human one, hallowed by so much blood, of 'our' assumed superiority, of 'their system' being 'repressive' or 'undemocratic' or of they – those 'others' – being 'backward' or 'uncivilized' and in need of being enlightened and 're-educated' by our 'progressive' ideas. Or, more probable, it would be some new standard or some new fashionable political or social or even religious dogma by which we commend ourselves on our progress and which we use, consciously or otherwise, to judge others by.

The current reality is that even if we had or soon established a terran 'prime directive' directing we humans not to interfere in the internal affairs of other humans here on Earth who are different, in whatever way, from ourselves, it is fairly certain it "would not be long before some human or some human authority, somewhere, manufactured some sly excuse to order to try and justify ignoring it..."

Which mention of a terran 'prime directive' leads to two of the other questions which cause me to vacillate between optimism and pessimism in regard to our future as a species. The question of increasing population, and the question of the finite resources of this Earth. Which suggests to me, as some others, that – especially as the majority of people now live in urban areas – a noble option is for us, as a species, to cooperate and betake ourselves to colonize our Moon, then Mars, and seek to develope such technology as would take us beyond our Solar System. For if we do not do this then the result would most probably be, at some future time, increasing conflict over land and resources, mass migrations (probably resulting in more conflict) and such governments or authorities as then exist forced by economic circumstance to adopt policies to reduce or limit their own population. Global problems probably exasperated still further by the detrimental changes that available evidence indicates could possibly result from what has been termed 'climate change' [6].

But is the beginning of this noble option of space colonization viable in the near future? Possibly not, given that the few countries that have the resources, the space expertise and the technology necessary – and the means to develope existing space technology – do not consider such exploration and colonization as a priority, existing as they seem to do in a world where nation-States still compete for influence and power and where conflict – armed, deadly, and otherwise – is still regarded as a viable solution to problems.

Which leads we human beings, with our jumelle character, confined to this small planet we call Earth, possibly continuing as we have, for millennia, continued: a quarrelsome species, often engaged (like primates) in minor territorial disputes; in our majority unempathic; often inconsiderate, often prejudiced (even though we like to believe otherwise); often inclined to place our self-interest and our pleasure first; often prone to being manipulated or to manipulating others; often addicted to the slyness of words spoken and written and heard and read; often believing 'we' are better than 'them'; and fighting, raping, hating, killing, invading here, interfering there. And beset by the problems wrought by increasing population, by dwindling resources, by mass migrations, by continuing armed conflicts (regional, local, supranational, over some-thing) and possibly also affected by the effects of climate change.

Yet also, sometimes despite ourselves, we are beings capable of – and have shown over millennia – compassion, kindness, gentleness, tolerance, love, fairness, reason, and a valourous self-sacrifice that is and has been inspirational. But perhaps above all we have, in our majority, exuded and kept and replenished the virtue of hope; hoping, dreaming, of better times, a better future, sometime, somewhere – and not, as it happens, for ourselves but for our children and their children and the future generations yet to be born. And it is this hope that changes us, and has changed us, for the better, as our human culture of pathei-mathos so eloquently, so numinously, and so tragically, reveals.

Thus the question seems to be whether we still have hope enough, dreams enough, nobility enough, and can find some way to change ourselves, to thus bring a better – a more fairer, more just, more compassionate – future into-being without causing or contributing to the suffering which so blights, and which has so blighted, our existence on Earth.

Personally, I am inclined to wonder if the way we need – the hope, the dream, we need – is that of setting forth to explore and colonize our Moon, then Mars, and then the worlds beyond our Solar System, guided by a prime directive.

2013
Revised 2017

Notes

[1] I understand 'the good' as what alleviates or does not cause suffering; what is compassionate; what is honourable; what is reasoned and balanced. Honour being here, and elsewhere in my recent writings, understood as the instinct for and an adherence to what is fair, dignified, and valourous.

[2] I have expanded, a little, on what I mean by 'the culture of pathei-mathos' in my tract *Questions of Good, Evil, Honour, and God*.

[3] As defined by my 'philosophy of pathei-mathos', I understand innocence as "an attribute of those who, being personally unknown to us, are therefore unjudged us by and who thus are given the benefit of the doubt. For this

presumption of innocence of others – until direct personal experience, and individual and empathic knowing of them, prove otherwise – is the fair, the reasoned, the numinous, the human, thing to do. Empathy and πάθει μάθος incline us toward treating other human beings as we ourselves would wish to be treated; that is they incline us toward fairness, toward self-restraint, toward being well-mannered, and toward an appreciation and understanding of innocence."

[4] Pœmandres (Corpus Hermeticum), 15 – διὰ τοῦτο παρὰ πάντα τὰ ἐπὶ γῆς ζῷα διπλοῦς ἐστιν ὁ ἄνθρωπος

As I noted in my translation of and commentary on the Pœmandres tract,

> "Jumelle. For διπλοῦς. The much underused and descriptive English word jumelle – from the Latin gemellus – describes some-thing made in, or composed of, two parts, and is therefore most suitable here, more so than common words such as 'double' or twofold."

[5] qv. Sophocles, Antigone, v.334, vv.365-366

> πολλὰ τὰ δεινὰ κοὐδὲν ἀνθρώπου δεινότερον πέλει...
> σοφόν τι τὸ μηχανόεν τέχνας ὑπὲρ ἐλπίδ᾽ ἔχων
> τοτὲ μὲν κακόν, ἄλλοτ᾽ ἐπ᾽ ἐσθλὸν ἕρπει

> There exists much that is strange, yet nothing
> Has more strangeness than a human being...
> Beyond his own hopes, his cunning
> In inventive arts – he who arrives
> Now with dishonour, then with chivalry

[6] Many people have a view about 'climate change' – for or against – for a variety of reasons. My own view is that the scientific evidence available at the moment seems to indicate that there is a change resulting from human activity and that this change could possibility be detrimental, in certain ways, to us and to the other life with which we share this planet. The expressions 'seems to indicate' and 'could possibly be' are necessary given that this view of mine might need to be, and should be, reassessed if and when new evidence or facts become available.

Persecution And War

A Remembering

Reared as a Roman Catholic, educated for a while at a Catholic preparatory school and then – again for a while – at a Catholic boarding school, I remember the history taught by our teachers and Priests of the centuries-long persecution of English and Irish Catholics that began in the 16th century. There were stories of martyrs; of recusants; of secret Masses; of anti-Catholic polemics and propaganda; and of the monks who – after the suppression of the monasteries, the theft of monastic lands and wealth, begun by a tyrannos named Henry – escaped to France and founded monasteries such as the one at Dieulouard in Lorraine.

There thus was engendered in we Catholic children a feeling of difference, aided by the fact that our Mass was in Latin, by our sacrament of confession, by the practice of Gregorian chant, and by the singing of hymns such as Faith Of Our Fathers with its memorable verses

> Faith of our Fathers living still
> In spite of dungeon, fire, and sword [...]
> We will be true to thee till death [...]
>
> Our Fathers, chained in prisons dark,
> Were still in heart and conscience free [...]
> Faith of our Fathers, Mary's prayers
> Shall win our country back to thee

This feeling of difference was forcefully remembered when I in the early 1970's – during The Troubles – ventured to visit Northern Ireland; when I in the mid-1970's and as a Catholic monk spent several weeks staying at a Presbytery in Dublin; and when I in the mid-1990's – before the Good Friday Agreement – visited Derry.

Forcefully remembered because I listened to accounts of the burning of Catholic homes by Protestant mobs in 1969 and the subsequent flight of hundreds of Catholic families to the Irish Republic where they were housed in refugee camps; listened to witness accounts of the killing of eleven Catholics, including a Priest, by the British Army in Ballymurphy in 1971; listened to witness accounts of the killing of fourteen Catholics, again by the British Army, in Derry in 1972; and listened to stories of the persecution of Irish Catholics under British rule.

Such a remembering, such a childhood feeling of difference, formed part of the years-long personal and philosophical reflexion that occupied me for several years as I, between 2006 and 2009, developed my 'numinous way' and then between 2011 and 2012 gradually refined it into the 'way of pathei-mathos', with the core of that reflexion concerning matters such as extremism, my own extremist past, war, prejudice, intolerance, and persecution.

War And Combat

Familiar as I was with ancient works by Thucydides, Herodotus, Livy, and others; with many works concerning more recent European history by modern historians, as well as with personal accounts of those who had fought for both the Allies and the Axis during World War Two, I recalled some words of Cicero:

> "Aliis ego te virtutibus, continentiae, gravitatis, iustitiae, fidei, ceteris omnibus."

> "because of your other virtues of self-restraint, of dignity, of fairness, of honesty, and all other such qualities..." [1]

Which led me to consider making a distinction between war and a more personal combat, between a modern *krieg* and the Old Germanic *werra*, given that war, from my reading of and admittedly fallible understanding of history, seemed to me to involve – by its very nature of necessitating killing and causing injury – intolerance, hatred, a divisive sense of difference often involving "us" believing we were "better" (or more civilized) than them, our enemies, thus leading to a dehumanization of "the enemy". A divisive sense of difference and a dehumanization often aided (particularly in modern times) by polemics, rumour, and propaganda; and a divisive sense of difference, a dehumanization, together with polemics, rumour, and propaganda, which I knew from my own decades of political and religious activism formed a core part of all types of extremism.

The distinction I considered was that personal combat unlike war did not involve large armies fighting against each other because of some diktat or personal agenda by some tyrannos or because of some ideology or religion or policy of some State or government. Instead, combat involved small groups – such as clans or tribes or neighbours – fighting because of some personal quarrel or some wrong or some perceived grievance.

But the more I considered this supposed distinction between combat and war the more I realized that in practice there was no such distinction since both involved principles similar to those of the Ancient Roman *Leges Regiae* – qv. the *Jus Papirianum* attributed to Sextus Papirius – where someone or some many possess or have acquired (through for example force of arms) or have assumed authority over others, and who by the use of violence and/or by the threat of punishment and/or by oratory or propaganda, are able to force or persuade others to accept such authority and obey the commands of such authority.

This acceptance by individuals of a supra-personal authority – or, more often, the demand by some supra-personal authority that individuals accept such a supra-personal authority – was manifest in the Christian writings of Augustine (b.354 CE, d.430 CE), such as his *De Civitate Dei contra Paganos* where in Book XIX, chapter xiii, he wrote of the necessity of a hierarchy in which God is the supreme authority, with peace between human beings and God requiring obedience to that authority; with peace between human beings, and civil peace, also of necessity requiring obedience to an order in which each person has their allotted place, "Ordo est parium disparium que rerum sua cuique loca tribuens dispositio."

Which hierarchy and acceptance of authority led Augustine to describe – in book XXII of *Contra Faustum Manichaeum* – the concept that war requires the authority of a person (such as a monarch) who has such "necessary" authority over others. This concept regarding war has remained a guiding principle of modern Western nations where the authority to inaugurate and prosecute a war against perceived enemies resides in the State, and thus in modern potentates who have seized power or in elected governments and their representatives such as Presidents and Prime Ministers.

Authority And Society

In the nations of the West, such a hierarchy of authority applies not only to war and its prosecution but also to changes, to reform, in society [2] for there is, as I mentioned in *The Numinous Way Of Pathei-Mathos*,

> "a hierarchy of judgement involved, whatever political 'flavour' the government is assigned to, is assumed to represent, or claims it represents; with this hierarchy of necessity requiring the individual in society to either (i) relinquish their own judgement, being accepting of or acquiescing in (from whatever reason or motive such as desire to avoid punishment) the judgement of these others, or (ii) to oppose this 'judgement of others' either actively through some group, association, or movement (political, social, religious) or individually, with there being the possibility that some so opposing this 'judgement of others' may resort to using violent means against the established order." [3]

In the way of pathei-mathos authority is personal, based on individual empathy and a personal pathei-mathos; both of which have a local horizon so that what is

> "beyond our personal empathic knowing of others, beyond our knowledge and our experience [our pathei-mathos], beyond the limited (local) range of our empathy and that personal (local) knowledge of ourselves which pathei-mathos reveals – is something we rationally, we humbly, accept we do not know and so cannot judge or form a reasonable, a fair, a balanced, opinion about. For empathy, like pathei-mathos, lives within us; manifesting, as both empathy and pathei-mathos do, the always limited nature, the horizon, of our own knowledge and understanding." [4]

In practical terms this means trying to cultivate within ourselves the virtues mentioned by Cicero – self-restraint, dignity, fairness, honesty – and implies we have no concern for or we seek to cultivate no concern for supra-personal hierarchies and supra-personal authority – whether political, religious, or otherwise – and thus move away from, try to distance ourselves from, the consequences of such supra-personal hierarchies and supra-personal authority manifest as the consequences are and have been, throughout our history, in war, prejudice, intolerance, unfairness, extremism, and persecution in the name of some ideology, some religion, or because someone has commanded us to persecute those that they and others have declared are "our" enemies, and which war and persecutions are often, especially in modern times, accompanied by propaganda and lies.

Thus in the case of my Catholic remembering, those soldiers in Ballymurphy and in Derry shot and killed civilians, women included, because those soldiers believed them to be "enemies", because propaganda had dehumanized those enemies; because those soldiers were part of and obeyed a hierarchical, supra-personal, chain-of-command by being there armed and prepared to use deadly force and violence against individuals they did not personally know; and because in the aftermath of those killings, and for years afterwards, they were not honest and hence did not contradict the propaganda stories, the lies, about those events which some of their superiors and others circulated in an attempt to justify such acts of inhumanity.

Yet for me the real tragedy is that events similar to those of my very personal remembering have occurred on a vaster scale millennia after millennia and are still occurring, again on a vaster scale and world-wide, despite us having access to the wisdom of the past, manifest as such wisdom is, for those reared in the West, in the Agamemnon of Aeschylus, in the Oedipus Tyrannus of Sophocles, in the mythos of Μοῖραι τρίμορφοι μνήμονές τ᾽ Ἐρινύες [5], in many of the writings of Cicero, in Τὰ εἰς ἑαυτόν by Marcus Aurelius, in the numinous beauty of Gregorian chant, in the music of JS Bach, and in so many, many, other writers and artists ancient and modern.

Ða sceolde se hearpere weorðan swa sarig
þæt he ne meahte ongemong oðrum mannum bion
(XXXV, 6)

9.ix.18

∘∘∘

[1] M. Tullius Cicero, *Pro Murena Oratio*, 23. My translation.

[2] By 'society' in the context of this essay and the way of pathei-mathos is meant a collection of individuals who dwell, who live, in a particular area and who are subject to the same laws and the same institutions of authority. Modern society is thus a manifestation of some State, and States are predicated on individuals actively or passively accepting some supra-personal authority, be it governmental (national) or regional (county), or more usually both.

[3] "Society, Politics, Social Reform, and Pathei-Mathos". *The Numinous Way Of Pathei-Mathos*. 2013. Fifth edition. Link: https://davidmyatt.files.wordpress.com/2018/03/numinous-way-v5c-print.pdf

[4] "Personal Reflexions On Some Metaphysical Questions." 2015. Link:

[5] "Trimorphed Moirai with their ever-heedful Furies." Aeschylus (attributed), Prometheus Bound, 516

The Matter With Death

The matter with death is that the flow of Life goes on, and we are just gone; simply gone from one planet orbiting one star in one galaxy among a universe of galaxies.

> No trains in the distant valley would stop...
> Only the cold day in Winter
> Might change
> Just a little
> When the sun shines into blue
> And white whisps of cirrus
> Gather to briefly signal the change

We just do not matter as much as we sometimes - often - believe or would like to believe, and all that we can hope for, perhaps, is that someone or some many may remember us, or that some compassionate deed of ours, some Presencing of The Numinous we had the fortune to presence in our life, may aid or help or have helped or aided some others in some way to live as we in the moments of our dying perhaps felt, remembered, we should have: born along by such nobility of personal love gently shared as made us reach out to where all our hopes and every Paradise, past-present-future, were born bringing such comfort and such beauty, such a wordless sense of goodness, that we in such moments became as happy children, again; there where no conflict touched us, no doubts assailed us, no hunger drained us, and no threats came to threaten or restrain.

> There was only the warming Sun as that morning when two new lovers, newly-born, betook themselves out to where a white sandy beach met with sea and where they swam swam together until tiredness came to bring them back to shore: no world beyond their world, there. Footprints soon washed away, by waveful sea.

So Life as Nature so presenced, here, will flow on: past our passing. To smooth out with durations of centuries our mistakes, our worries, doubts and fears, and such interference as perhaps so kept us once suffused with a passion and sometimes manipulation and lies, born from bloated self-importance and the delusive ideation of individual Change.

For there is no destiny that comes to shake, mould, preen and make us: only the flow that carries us while we with our illusion of self so lasts. All we are, are moments, passing: as the falling leaf of Autumn falls, having lost its Springful green, no one there to blame.

We just do not matter as we hope, believe, or would like to believe, we do: for there is no you or I or we to hold us here. Only one Life, presenced, here and growing, flowing - one Earth turning where one Sun lights one small part of our greater cosmic dark.

August 2011

Appendix I

Physis And Being
An Introduction To The Philosophy Of Pathei-Mathos

The philosophy of pathei-mathos is based on four axioms: (i) that it is empathy and pathei-mathos which can wordlessly reveal the ontological reality both of our own physis [1] and of how we, as sentient beings, relate to other living beings and to Being itself; (ii) that it is denotatum [2] – and thus the abstractions deriving therefrom [3] – which, in respect of human beings, can and often do obscure our physis and our relation to other living beings and to Being; (iii) that denotatum and abstractions imply a dialectic of contradictory opposites and thus for we human beings a separation-of-otherness; and (iv) that this dialectic of opposites is, has been, and can be a cause of suffering for both ourselves, as sentient beings, and – as a causal human presenced effect – for the other life with which we share the planet named in English as Earth.

For, as mentioned in a previous essay,

> "empathy and pathei-mathos incline us to suggest that ipseity is an
> illusion of perspective: that there is, fundamentally, no division
> between 'us' – as some individual sentient, mortal being – and what
> has hitherto been understood and named as the Unity, The One, God,
> The Eternal. That 'we' are not 'observers' but rather Being existing as
> Being exists and is presenced in the Cosmos. That thus all our
> striving, individually and collectively when based on some ideal or on
> some form – some abstraction and what is derived therefrom, such as
> ideology and dogma – always is or becomes sad/tragic, and which

recurrence of sadness/tragedy, generation following generation, is perhaps even inevitable unless and until we live according to the wordless knowing that empathy and pathei-mathos reveal." [4]

In essence, empathy and pathei-mathos lead us away from the abstractions we have constructed and manufactured and which abstractions we often tend to impose, or project, upon other human beings, upon ourselves, often in the belief that such abstractions can aid our understanding of others and of ourselves, with a feature of all abstractions being inclusion and exclusion; that is, certain individuals are considered as belonging to or as defined by a particular category while others are not.

Over millennia we have manufactured certain abstractions and their assumed opposites and classified many of them according to particular moral standards so that a particular abstraction is considered good and/or beneficial and/or as necessary and/or as healthy, while its assumed dialectical opposite is considered bad (or evil), or unnecessary, or unhealthy, and/or as unwarranted.

Thus in ancient Greece and Rome slavery was accepted by the majority, and considered by the ruling elite as natural and necessary, with human beings assigned to or included in the category 'slave' a commodity who could be traded with slaves regarded as necessary to the functioning of society. Over centuries, with the evolution of religions such as Christianity and with the development in Western societies of humanist weltanschauungen, the moral values of this particular abstraction, this particular category to which certain human beings assigned, changed such that for perhaps a majority slavery came to be regarded as morally repugnant. Similarly in respect of the abstraction designated in modern times by such terms as "the rôle of women in society" which rôle for millennia in the West was defined according to various masculous criteria – deriving from a ruling and an accepted patriarchy – but which rôle in the past century in Western societies has gradually been redefined.

Yet irrespective of such developments, such changes associated with certain abstractions, the abstractions themselves and the dialectic of moral opposites associated with them remain because, for perhaps a majority, abstractions and ipseity, as a criteria of judgment and/or as a human instinct, remain; as evident in the continuing violence against, the killing of, and the manipulation, of women by men, and in what has become described by terms such as "modern slavery" and "human trafficking".

In addition, we human beings have continued to manufacture abstractions and continue to assign individuals to them, a useful example being the abstraction denoted by the terms The State and The Nation-State [5] and which abstraction, with its government, its supra-personal authority, its laws, its economy, and its inclusion/exclusion (citizenship or lack of it) has come to dominate and influence the life of the majority of people in the West.

Ontologically, abstractions – ancient and modern – usurp our connexion to Being and to other living beings so that instead of using wordless empathy and pathei-mathos as a guide to Reality [6] we tend to define ourselves or are defined by others according to an abstraction or according to various abstractions. In the matter of the abstraction that is The State there is a tendency to define or to try to understand our relation to Reality by for example whether we belong, are a citizen of a particular State; by whether or not we have an acceptable standard of living because of the opportunities and employment and/or the assistance afforded by the economy and the policies of the State; by whether or not we agree or disagree with the policies of the government in power, and often by whether or not we have transgressed some State-made law or laws. Similarly, in the matter of belief in a revealed religion such as Christianity or Islam we tend to define or understand our relation to Reality by means of such an abstraction: that is, according to the revelation (or a particular interpretation of it) and its eschatology, and thus by how the promise of Heaven/Jannah may be personally obtained.

Empathy and pathei-mathos, however, wordlessly – sans denotatum, sans abstractions, sans a dialectic of contradictory opposites – uncover physis: our physis, that of other mortals, that of other living beings, and that of Being/Reality itself. Which physis, howsoever presenced – in ourselves, in other living beings, in Being – is fluxive, a balance between the being that it now is, that it was, and that it has the inherent (the acausal) quality to be. [7]

This uncovering, such a revealing, is of a knowing beyond ipseity and thus beyond the separation-of-otherness which denotatum, abstractions, and a dialectic of opposites manufacture and presence. A knowing of ourselves as an affective connexion [8] to other living beings and to Being itself, with Being revealed as fluxive (as a meson – μέσον [9] – with the potentiality to change, to develope) and thus which (i) is not – as in the theology of revealed religions such as Christianity and Islam – a God who is Eternal, Unchanging, Omnipotent [10], and (ii) is affected or can be affected (in terms of physis) by what we do or do not do.

This awareness, this knowing, of such an affective connexion – our past, our current, our potentiality, to adversely affect, to have adversely affected, to cause, to having caused, suffering or harm to other living beings – also inclines us or can incline us toward benignity and humility, and thus incline us to live in a non-suffering causing way, appreciate of our thousands of years old culture of pathei-mathos. [11]

In terms of understanding Being and the divine, it inclines us or can incline us, as sentient beings, to apprehend Being as not only presenced in us but as capable of changing – unfolding, evolving – in a manner dependant on our physis and on how our physis is presenced by us, and by others, in the future. Which seems to imply a new ontology and one distinct from past and current theologies with their anthropomorphic θεὸς (god) and θεοὶ (gods).

An ontology of physis: of mortals, of livings beings, and of Being, as fluxive mesons. Of we mortals as a mortal microcosm of Being – the cosmic order, the κόσμος – itself [12] with the balance, the meson, that empathy and pathei-mathos incline us toward living presenced in the ancient Greek phrase καλὸς κἀγαθός,

> "which means those who conduct themselves in a gentlemanly or lady-like manner and who thus manifest – because of their innate physis or through pathei-mathos or through a certain type of education or learning – nobility of character." [13]

Which personal conduct, in the modern world, might suggest a Ciceronian-inspired but new type of *civitas*, and one

> "not based on some abstractive law but on a spiritual and interior (and thus not political) understanding and appreciation of our own Ancestral Culture and that of others; on our 'civic' duty to personally presence καλὸς κἀγαθός and thus to act and to live in a noble way. For the virtues of personal honour and manners, with their responsibilities, presence the fairness, the avoidance of hubris, the natural harmonious balance, the gender equality, the awareness and appreciation of the divine, that is the numinous." [14]

With καλὸς κἀγαθός, such personal conduct, and such a new civitas, summarising how the philosophy of pathei-mathos might, in one way, be presenced in a practical manner in the world.

2019

°°°

Notes

[1] I use the term physis – φύσις – ontologically, in the Aristotelian sense, to refer to the 'natural' and the fluxive being (nature) of a being, which nature is often manifest, in we mortals, in our character (persona) and in our deeds. Qv. my essay *Towards Understanding Physis* (2015) and my translation of and commentary on the Poemandres tractate in *Corpus Hermeticum: Eight Tractates* (2017).

[2] As noted elsewhere, I use the term denotatum – from the Latin denotare – not only as meaning "to denote or to describe by an expression or a word; to name some-thing; to refer that which is so named or so denoted," but also as an Anglicized term implying, depending on context, singular or plural instances. As an Anglicized term there is generally no need to use the inflected plural *denotata*.

[3] In the context of the philosophy of pathei-mathos the term abstraction signifies a particular named and defined category or form (ἰδέα, εἶδος) and which category or form is a manufactured generalization, a hypothesis, a posited thing, an assumption or assumptions about, an extrapolation of or from some-thing, or some assumed or extrapolated ideal 'form' of some-thing.

In respect of denotatum, in Kratylus 389d Plato has Socrates talk about 'true, ideal' naming (denotatum) – βλέποντα πρὸς αὐτὸ ἐκεῖνο ὃ ἔστιν ὄνομα, qv. my essay *Personal Reflexions On Some Metaphysical Questions*, 2015.

[4] *Personal Reflexions On Some Metaphysical Questions*.

[5] Contrary to modern convention I tend to write The State instead of "the state" because I consider The State/The Nation-State a particular abstraction; as an existent, an entity, which has been manufactured, by human beings, and which entity, like many such manufactured 'things', has been, in its design and function, changed and which can still be changed, and which has associated with it a presumption of a supra-personal (and often moral) authority.

In addition, written The State (or the State) it suggests some-thing which endures or which may endure beyond the limited lifespan of a mortal human being.

[6] 'Reality' in the philosophical sense of what (in terms of physis) is distinguished or distinguishable from what is apparent or external. In terms of ancient Hellenic and Western Renaissance mysticism the distinction is between the esoteric and the exoteric; between the physis of a being and some outer form (or appearance) including the outer form that is a useful tool or implement which can be used to craft or to manufacture some-thing such as other categories/abstractions. With the important ontological proviso that what is esoteric is not the 'essence' of something – as for example Plato's ἰδέα/εἶδος – but instead the physis of the being itself as explicated for instance by Aristotle in Metaphysics, Book 5, 1015α,

> ἐκ δὴ τῶν εἰρημένων ἡ πρώτη φύσις καὶ κυρίως λεγομένη ἐστὶν ἡ οὐσία ἡ τῶν ἐχόντων ἀρχὴν κινήσεως ἐν αὐτοῖς ᾗ αὐτά: ἡ γὰρ ὕλη τῷ ταύτης δεκτικὴ εἶναι λέγεται φύσις, καὶ αἱ γενέσεις καὶ τὸ φύεσθαι τῷ ἀπὸ ταύτης εἶναι κινήσεις. καὶ ἡ ἀρχὴ τῆς κινήσεως τῶν φύσει ὄντων αὕτη ἐστίν, ἐνυπάρχουσά πως ἢ δυνάμει ἢ ἐντελεχείᾳ

> Given the foregoing, then principally – and to be exact – physis denotes the quidditas of beings having changement inherent within them; for substantia has been denoted by physis because it embodies this, as have the becoming that is a coming-into-being, and a burgeoning, because they are changements predicated on it. For physis is inherent changement either manifesting the potentiality of a being or as what a being, complete of itself, is.

That is, as I noted in my essay *Towards Understanding Physis*, it is a meson (μέσον) balanced between the being that-it-was and the being it has the potentiality to unfold to become.

In respect of "what is real" – τῶν ὄντων – cf. the Poemandres tractate of the Corpus Hermeticum and especially section 3,

> φημὶ ἐγώ, Μαθεῖν θέλω τὰ ὄντα καὶ νοῆσαι τὴν τούτων φύσιν καὶ γνῶναι τὸν θεόν
>
> I answered that I seek to learn what is real, to apprehend the physis of beings, and to have knowledge of theos [qv. *Corpus Hermeticum: Eight Tractates*, 2017]

[7] Qv. *Towards Understanding Physis*, 2015.

[8] I use the term *affective* here, and in other writings, to mean "having the quality of affecting; tending to affect or influence."

[9] Qv. footnote [6]. In terms of ontology a meson is the balance, the median, existing between the being which-was and the being which-can-be.

[10] This understanding of Being as fluxive – as a changement – was prefigured in the mythos of Ancient Greece with the supreme deity – the chief of the gods – capable of being overthrown and replaced, as Zeus overthrew Kronos and as Kronos himself overthrew his own father.

[11] As explained in my 2014 essay *Education And The Culture of Pathei-Mathos*, the term describes "the accumulated pathei-mathos of individuals, world-wide, over thousands of years, as (i) described in memoirs, aural stories, and historical accounts; as (ii) have inspired particular works of literature or poetry or drama; as (iii) expressed via non-verbal mediums such as music and Art, and as (iv) manifest in more recent times by 'art-forms' such as films and documentaries."

This culture remembers the suffering and the beauty and the killing and the hubris and the love and the compassion that we mortals have presenced and caused over millennia, and which culture

> "thus includes not only traditional accounts of, or accounts inspired by, personal pathei-mathos, old and modern – such as the *With The Old Breed: At Peleliu and Okinawa* by Eugene Sledge, *One Day in the Life of Ivan Denisovich* by Aleksandr Solzhenitsyn, and the poetry of people as diverse as Sappho and Sylvia Plath – but also works or art-forms inspired by such pathei-mathos, whether personal or otherwise, and whether factually presented or fictionalized. Hence films such as *Monsieur Lazhar* and *Etz Limon* may poignantly express something about our φύσις as human beings and thus form part of the

culture of pathei-mathos."

[12] κόσμον δὲ θείου σώματος κατέπεμψε τὸν ἄνθρωπον, "a cosmos of the divine body sent down as human beings." Tractate IV:2, Corpus Hermeticum.

Cf. Marsilii Ficini, *De Vita Coelitus Comparanda*, XXVI, published in 1489 CE,

> Quomodo per inferiora superioribus exposita deducantur superiora, et per mundanas materias mundana potissimum dona.

> How, when what is lower is touched by what is higher, the higher is cosmically presenced therein and thus gifted because cosmically aligned.

Which is a philosophical restatement of the phrase "quod est inferius est sicut quod est superius" (what is above is as what is below) from the Latin version, published in 1541 CE, of the medieval Hermetic text known as *Tabula Smaragdina*.

[13] The quotation is from my *Classical Paganism And The Christian Ethos*, 2017.

[14] The quotation is from my *Tu Es Diaboli Ianua: Christianity, The Johannine Weltanschauung, And Presencing The Numinous*, 2017.

Appendix II

Pathei-Mathos: Genesis of My Unknowing

There are no excuses for my extremist past, for the suffering I caused to loved ones, to family, to friends, to those many more, those far more, 'unknown others' who were or who became the 'enemies' posited by some extremist ideology. No excuses because the extremism, the intolerance, the hatred, the violence, the inhumanity, the prejudice were mine; my responsibility, born from and expressive of my character; and because the discovery of, the learning of, the need to live, to regain, my humanity arose because of and from others and not because of me.

Thus what exposed my hubris - what for me broke down that certitude-of-knowing which extremism breeds and re-presents - was not something I did; not something I achieved; not something related to my character, my nature, at all. Instead, it was a gift offered to me by two others - the legacy left by their tragic early dying. That it took not one but two personal tragedies - some thirteen years apart - for me to accept and appreciate the gift of their love, their living, most surely reveals my failure, the hubris that for so long suffused me, and the strength and depth of my so lamentable extremism.

But the stark and uneasy truth is that I have no real, no definitive, answers for anyone, including myself. All I have now is a definite uncertitude of knowing, and certain feelings, some intuitions, some reflexions, a few certainly fallible suggestions arising mostly from reflexions concerning that, my lamentable, past, and thus - perhaps - just a scent, just a scent, of some understanding concerning some-things, perfumed as this understanding is with ineffable sadness.

For what I painfully, slowly, came to understand, via pathei-mathos, was the importance - the human necessity, the virtue - of love, and how love expresses or can express the numinous in the most sublime, the most human, way. Of how extremism (of whatever political or religious or ideological kind) places some abstraction, some ideation, some notion of duty to some ideation, before a personal love, before a knowing and an appreciation of the numinous. Thus does extremism - usurping such humanizing personal love - replace human love with an extreme, an unbalanced, an intemperate, passion for something abstract: some ideation, some ideal, some dogma, some 'victory', some-thing always supra-personal and always destructive of personal happiness, personal dreams, personal hopes; and always manifesting an impersonal harshness: the harshness of hatred, intolerance, certitude-of-knowing, unfairness, violence, prejudice.

Thus, instead of a natural and a human concern with what is local, personal and personally known, extremism breeds a desire to harshly interfere in the lives of others - personally unknown and personally distant - on the basis of such a hubriatic certitude-of-knowing that strife and suffering are inevitable. For there is in all extremists that stark lack of personal humility, that unbalance, that occurs when - as in all extremisms - what is masculous is emphasized and idealized and glorified to the detriment (internal, and external) of what is muliebral, and thus when some ideology or some dogma or some faith or some cause is given precedence over love and when loyalty to some manufactured abstraction is given precedence over loyalty to family, loved ones, friends.

For I have sensed that there are only changeable individual ways and individual fallible answers, born again and again via pathei-mathos and whose subtle scent - the wisdom - words can neither capture nor describe, even though we try and perhaps need to try, and try perhaps (as for me) as one hopeful needful act of a non-religious redemption.

Thus, and for instance, I sense - only sense - that peace (or the beginning thereof) might possibly just be not only the freedom from subsuming personal desires but also the freedom from striving for some supra-personal, abstract, impersonal, goal or goals. That is, a just-being, a flowing and a being-flowed. No subsuming concern with what-might-be or what-was. No lust for ideations; no quest for the violation of difference. Instead - a calmful waiting; just a listening, a seeing, a feeling, of what-is as those, as our, emanations of Life flow and change as they naturally flow and change, in, with, and beyond us: human, animal, of sea, soil, sky, Cosmos, and of Nature... But I am only dreaming, here in pathei-mathos-empathy-land where there is no past-present-future passing each of us with our future-past: only the numen presenced in each one of our so individual timeless human stories.

Yet, in that - this - other world, the scent of having understood remains, which is why I feel I now quite understand why, in the past, certain individuals disliked - even hated - me, given my decades of extremism: my advocacy of racism, fascism, holocaust denial, and National-Socialism, followed (after my conversion to Islam) by my support of bin Laden, the Taliban, and advocacy of 'suicide attacks'.

I also understand why - given my subversive agenda and my amoral willingness to use any tactic, from Occult honeytraps to terrorism, to undermine the society of the time as prelude to revolution - certain people have saught to discredit me by distributing and publishing certain allegations.

Furthermore, given my somewhat Promethean peregrinations - which included being a Catholic monk, a vagabond, a fanatical violent neo-nazi, a theoretician of terror, running a gang of thieves, studying Buddhism, Hinduism, Taoism; being a nurse, a farm worker, and supporter of Jihad - I expect many or most of those interested in or curious about my 'numinous way' and my recent mystical writings to be naturally suspicious of or doubtful about my reformation and my rejection of extremism.

Thus I harbour no resentment against individuals, or organizations, or groups, who over the past forty or so years have publicly and/or privately made negative or derogatory comments about me or published items making claims about me. Indeed, I now find myself in the rather curious situation of not only agreeing with some of my former political opponents on many matters, but also (perhaps) of understanding (and empathizing with) their motivation; a situation which led and which leads me to appreciate even more just how lamentable my extremism was and just how arrogant, selfish, wrong, and reprehensible, I as a person was, and how in many ways many of those former opponents were and are (*ex concesso*) better people than I ever was or am.

Which is one reason why I have written what I have recently written about extremism and my extremist past: so that perchance someone or some many may understand extremism, and its causes, better and thus be able to avoid the mistakes I made, avoid causing the suffering I caused; or be able to in some way more effectively counter or prevent such extremism in the future. And one reason - only one - why I henceforward must live in reclusion and *in silencio.*

May 2012

In Loving Memory of Frances, died 29th May 2006
In Loving Memory of Sue, died 4th April 1993

Appendix III

A Matter of Honour

Given the persistence of unsubstantiated rumours and allegations regarding involvement with Occultism, I deemed it necessary to publicly comment, in some detail, about the matter and thus provide 'my side of the story' to compliment my autobiography *Myngath*.

However, as I note here in the conclusion, even though the matter is one of honour I do not expect the plethora of rumours and allegations to suddenly cease as a result of such comments by me, although I perhaps naively nurture a vague hope that what I write here may cause a few individuals to reconsider the veracity of such rumours and allegations.

March 5th, 2012
(Revised December 2012)

Journalists, Allegations, and Propaganda

For many years – in fact up to and including the present – rumours and allegations concerning my involvement with practical occultism and satanism have been in circulation, and regularly referred to and repeated by journalists, and others, in newspapers, magazines, articles and, latterly, on that new medium - greatly susceptible to the spreading of dishonourable allegations and rumours - that has been termed the Internet. One of these allegations is that I am a certain person known as Anton Long.

In the past thirty-seven years only four people, on hearing or learning about such rumours and allegations, have had the decency to ask me, in person, "for my side of the story". The first was Colin Jordan, the second was John Tyndall, the third was Steve Sargent, and the fourth was a Muslim whom I came to greatly admire and to whom I gave a personal pledge of loyalty.

I have, when asked in person, or via impersonal means of communication such as letters, always denied such allegations of such involvement, as I have, on numerous occasions, challenged anyone to provide evidence to support such accusations. No such evidence has ever been forthcoming [1].

For instance, I was for several days, in early 2000, covertly filmed, photographed, and followed by an investigative team working for the BBC as part of their research for a Panorama programme about David Copeland and the London nail-bombings [2]. Prior to that surveillance, and for an ever longer period, I was also the subject of covert surveillance by a private investigator hired to undertake preliminary research for that BBC investigation. What did all this covert surveillance and investigation reveal? A satanist? No. Someone living an ordinary, rather boring, life with his wife and family in a small village near Malvern who went to work everyday on a bicycle to a nearby farm.

In addition, since at least 1997 I have no doubt been under regular covert surveillance by Special Branch and MI5 – and especially so since 9/11 given some statements I made while a Muslim - with all my communications (internet, telephonic) monitored via GCHQ. Indeed, following my conversion to Islam and during the time I seemed to be, for the security services and the Police, 'a significant person of interest', I recall many meetings and friendly conversations with one of the Special Branch officers on attachment to the city near where I was then living.

Given such surveillance and interest, no doubt there are records somewhere of my activities as a neo-nazi extremist; of my subsequent life as a radical Muslim supporting Jihad, and finally of my life as a reclusive philosopher, a friend of σοφόν who seeks, through λόγος, to uncover – to understand – Being and beings, and who thus suggests or proposes an ontology of Being. What there will not be, will be any records of 'Myatt as Satanist'.

As I mentioned in my article *Polemos Our Genesis* in respect of such surveillance:

> "I have [since at least 1997] worked on the assumption that my communications are monitored, so I have restricted my internet and telephonic communications to friends, family, and to people I personally know or who are personally known to someone I trust. This means two things. That all I communicate is personal, open, transparent, and honest; and that if someone not belonging to this small circle of contacts claims to have had some communication from me – either sent with my name or sent using some pseudonym – then it is bogus."

In respect of rumours and allegations, I have, on a few occasions, challenged some individuals to a duel with deadly weapons, according to the etiquette of duelling. Not one of the individuals so challenged to a duel had the honour to accept, or issue a public apology in lieu of fighting such a duel.

As I wrote some thirteen or more years ago:

> " I have never bothered to have recourse to civil law, and established Courts, to sue those making libellous allegations about me quite simply because the only law I believe in and strive to uphold is the law of personal honour. Given that I have challenged two journalists, according to the law of personal honour, to a duel with deadly weapons for making such malicious allegations, and given that they did not have the honour to accept this challenge or issue an apology in lieu of fighting a duel, I consider my honour vindicated."

Such challenges, the lack of evidence to support the allegations and rumours, and the refusal of those so challenged to a duel of honour to either fight that duel of honour or issue an apology, reveals the truth of this particular matter – at least to those possessed of arête.

However, I quite understand why many people - journalists included - did in the past (and possibly still do) impersonally dislike or hate me, given my past and unethical support for, and my past propagation of neo-nazism, and my previous lamentable public incitement of hatred, intolerance, and violence. I was only reaping what I had sown. Thus I believe I also understand the motivation of those journalists and those authors who used rumours and allegations of involvement with Satanism to discredit me, for they were most probably only doing what they thought was necessary in the struggle against racism, extremism, and bigotry. But does that struggle - for what is ethical - justify their (in my view) unethical use of rumours and unproven allegations?

My own rather old-fashioned view is and was that a personal knowing of someone, extending over a period of many months if not a year or more, is the only honourable way to form a reasoned opinion about someone. For honour means the cultivation of traditional gentlemanly and ladylike virtues and one of which virtues is that we strive to treat other human beings in a fair way; ignoring what others have said or written about them; ignoring their past (real or alleged); and giving them the benefit of the doubt unless and until direct personal experience, direct knowledge of them, reveals them to be dishonourable.

Instead of penning material based on such a personal knowing, it occurs to me that some journalists who wrote and published stories about me might knowingly or unknowingly have or had a somewhat prejudiced view, having put some political or personal agenda before veracity, and thence use their position and/or their influence (use the power of the Media) to propagate their opinion, their version of events, and belittle or otherwise denigrate persons they disliked or did not approve of because they viewed that person not in an empathic, non-judgemental way - as an individual human being whom they had taken the trouble to get to know - but in an impersonal abstract way according to some label or category they had assigned to that individual because of the alleged political or religious views of that individual. Thus, in my own case, they prejudged me - categorized me - as a 'fascist' or a 'nazi' or a 'satanist' - and since they disliked or hated fascists and nazis and considered satanists were immoral and 'evil', they adjudged me a reprehensible person whom they did not like.

Furthermore, in place of a personal knowing - and/or a scholarly research into the life and times of the person they intend to write about and lasting many months if not a year or more - they rely on certain journalistic practices in order to gather information. Practices such as: (1) bribing or persuading corrupt Police officers and government officials and others in order to obtain confidential information about individuals; (2) hacking/intercepting people's private telephonic/internet communications; (3) hiring private investigators to follow individuals and gather information about them; (4) hypocritically attempting to excuse such unethical conduct by making the spurious claim that what they write or say is 'in the public interest' when not only is this so-called 'public interest' an unethical abstraction but also when they as individuals would be offended if someone used such hack journalistic practices against them and their own family. Thus, and for example, a well-known anti-fascist organization could unethically obtain confidential information about its opponents by getting someone sympathetic to their cause in the civil service to obtain national insurance numbers, dates of birth, places of residence, and employment history; as they could employ the services of an unethical private investigator to obtain that and other information via corrupt officials and by covert surveillance.

The result of such journalistic practices, of such a lack of personal knowing, of such a lack of scholarly research, and of such prejudgement of a person, is a hasty piece of work that - to paraphrase what a friend of mine once wrote - possibly says more about the journalist, more about our society, and more about the modern Media, that it does about the person who is the subject of such a piece of work.

In addition, and importantly, are those who in the past have prejudged me - who have written about me as a violent extremist - accepting of individual change, of the virtues of reformation and pardonance? Are they aware of my voluminous recent writings regarding my philosophy of pathei-mathos and those regarding my extremist past and my rejection of extremism? [3] Are they open to the possibility of my change and reformation? Or will they continue with 'the party line' and thus continue to insist that I am some sinister person whose recent mystical writings are just some sort of diabolical ploy?

More interestingly (perhaps) could my career as an extremist have been brought to an earlier end had one or some of my opponents taken the trouble to get to know me personally and rationally revealed to me the error of my suffering-causing, unethical, extremist ways? Perhaps; perhaps not - I admit I do not know. I do know, however, how my personal interaction with, and the ethical behaviour of, the Police I interacted with from the time of my arrest by officers from SO12 in 1998, permanently changed (for the better) my attitude toward the Police.

The Logical Fallacy of Incomplete Evidence - A Case Study

In a Master of Arts thesis entitled *Political Esotericism & the convergence of Radical Islam, Satanism and National Socialism in the Order of the Nine Angles* a post-graduate student named Senholt made certain claims, and drew certain conclusions, in respect of myself and alleged involvement with the Occult group the 'order of nine angles'. One of his claims is that "the role of David Myatt is paramount to the whole creation and existence of the ONA."

Given that this thesis [4] is often cited as having 'proved' my involvement, I believe a brief overview of the claims, and proofs offered, seems to be in order, especially as - to my knowledge - it has not so far been subjected to a critical analysis.

A reading of the thesis reveals two interesting things. First, the use of and reliance upon secondary and tertiary sources, many of which are anonymous and many of which are derived from 'the world wide web', that most unreliable source of information. For example, he relies on the book *Black Sun* by Goodrick-Clarke even after admitting it contains errors and that the author offers no proof for the assumptions made in respect of me and the ONA [5].

Second, that Senholt, undoubtedly inadvertently, commits the logical fallacy of incomplete evidence [6]. That is, the multitude of facts and circumstances which do not support his contention about me and the ONA are omitted.

Thus, and in my view, the Senholt thesis, while interesting, does not meet the requirement, the criteria, of scholarship.

This criteria is essentially two-fold: (i) of detailed, meticulous, unbiased research on and concerning a specific topic or topics or subject undertaken over a period of some considerable time, usually a year or more in duration, and of necessity involving primary source material; and (ii) a rational assessment of the knowledge acquired by such research, with such conclusions about the topic, topics, or subject therefore being not only the logical result of the cumulative scholarly learning so acquired but also possessing a certain gravitas, just like genuine scholars.

His lack of primary research is evident in several factual errors. A few examples:

(1) He repeats Searchlight's claim that their 'expose' of me in the April 1998 issue of their magazine caused internal strife in the National Socialist groups I was then involved with, whereas it had no effect at all, other than to make people laugh, since few if anyone of the extremists in such groups ever took seriously anything stated in *Searchlight*. Instead, as their name for it indicated - *Searchlies* - they regarded it as "just more Jewish propaganda" and indeed as something of a badge of honour to be mentioned in it, with the general feeling being that 'if you get mentioned in *Searchlies* you must be doing something right!'

(2) He asserts that in 1998 the Police raided my home and arrested me. Which is correct. He then asserts that I was arrested again two years later, after the London nailbomb attacks, together with some other Combat 18 members. Which is incorrect. The facts being that I was not arrested in 2000, and that the 1998 raids were the ones that also involved some C18 and NSM members.

(3) He writes that: "His conversion did not escape the mainstream media, and most English newspapers and media-outlets wrote about the incident, including the BBC." In fact, as a search of media archives would have revealed, my conversion in 1998 was never mentioned until two years after the fact, and most of the media publicity in 2000 linking me with Copeland made no mention of it. But perhaps Senholt just meant to write something along the lines of 'the fact that Myatt was, at the time of Copeland's trial, a Muslim did not escape some of the mainstream media...'

Moving on to his claims that there are several things which link me with the ONA. All of these alleged links can be shown not only to be unsupported by the facts but also that they do not even amount, as Senholt states, to circumstantial evidence in support of the claim made that I am Anton Long. The claims are:

(1) The use of alternative dating systems, such as yf, by both me and the ONA.

The fact that group A and group B use the same or a similar alternative dating system is not proof that B is a subset of A, only of borrowing, imitation, adaptation, and possibly of plagiarism.

(2) Some occult texts with my name on them.

See the first part of 'omitted facts and circumstances', below - regarding using the occult as a neo-nazi honeytrap.

(3) That ONA insight roles included supporting neo-nazi groups and terrorism (neo-nazi and Islamic), things which I was openly involved with.

As with alternative dating systems and some ideas (such as acausality - see item (5) below) there is only a possible borrowing, imitation, adaptation, plagiarism.

Also, what is not mentioned are the other ONA insight roles which do not fit in with my life. Such as a police officer, assassin, and joining an anarchist group.

(4) That there is linguistic evidence linking my writings and those of 'Anton Long'.

No evidence from forensic linguistics is presented, so that this claim is just claim about two people using similar concepts and ideas and sometimes the same words.

That is, there is no direct evidence of a link, so that once again this is probably just others borrowing, imitating and adapting already existing ideas and concepts, something that, like plagiarism, happens all the time.

(5) That my departure from Islam (in 2009) coincided with 'Anton Long' writing a plethora of new ONA items.

Since Senholt does not give dates, and does not list the items, before and after this date, this is a rather vague assumption which also ignores two important facts. First, the vast quantity of literature I produced from 2006 onwards (following the suicide of my fiancée) in the form of essays about my Numinous Way/philosophy of pathei-mathos, letters, poetry, and so on. Second, Senholt does not discuss the fact that there were and are several self-confessed satanists (such as the pseudonymous Jason King) who are of opinion that most if not all of the newer, recent, items attributed to Anton Long were written by someone quite different from the 'original Anton Long' associated with the original ONA (or ONA 1.0 as King described it).

(6) That some of my ideas and concepts - such as acausality and Aeons and Homo Galactica - are and have been used by the ONA.

These concepts date to the early to middle 1970's, evident in such non-occult writings as *Emanations of Urania*, and, later on, in my *Vindex - Destiny of the West*.

As an early advocate of copyleft, I have never been bothered by plagiarism or by others using and adapting my ideas and my 'inventions', such as The Star Game. Thus there is use and adaptation by others, and possibly plagiarism, but no proof of a direct link.

In most of the above cases there is also the established and the admitted fact up until 1998 I knew, as friends, some of the people involved with various occult groups, although - as mentioned to Professor Kaplan [7] and others - I did not share their views with us therefore agreeing to disagree on many things. Thus some allowed borrowing of ideas, concepts, and inventions, by such friends is hardly surprising.

Finally, the omitted facts and circumstances that do not support Senholt's claims and conclusions include:

(1) My publicly stated admission, made in the 1990's in correspondence with Professor Kaplan and others - and publicly repeated by me many times in the past ten and more years - that my occult involvement, such as it was in the 1970's and later, was for the singular purpose of subversion and infiltration in the cause of National-Socialism, with part of this being to spread racist ideas and denial of the holocaust. Thus one such occult group I associated with was a honeytrap, and the whole intent was political, revolutionary, not occult and not to with 'satanism'. It was a matter of using, or trying to use, such occult groups for a specific neo-nazi purpose without any interest in or personal involvement with the occult.

As I wrote in part two (1973-1975) of *Ethos of Extremism*:

> "In respect of covert action, I came to the conclusion, following some discussions with some C88 members, that two different types of covert groups, with different strategy and tactics, might be very useful in our struggle and thus aid us directly or aid whatever right-wing political party might serve as a cover for introducing NS policies or which could be used to advance our cause. These covert groups would not be paramilitary and thus would not resort to using armed force since that option was already covered, so far as I was then concerned, by C88.
>
> The first type of covert group would essentially be a honeytrap, to attract non-political people who might be or who had the potential to be useful to the cause even if, or especially if, they had to be 'blackmailed' or persuaded into doing so at some future time. The second type of covert group would be devoted to establishing a small cadre of NS fanatics, of 'sleepers', to - when the time was right - be disruptive or generally subversive.
>
> Nothing came of this second idea, and the few people I recruited during 1974 for the second group, migrated to help the first group, established the previous year. However, from the outset this first group was beset with problems for - in retrospect - two quite simple reasons, both down to me. First, my lack of leadership skills, and, second, the outer nature chosen for the group which was of a secret Occult group with the 'offer', the temptation, of sexual favours from female members in a ritualized Occult setting, with some of these female members being 'on the game' and associated with someone who was associated with my small gang of thieves [...]
>
> But what happened was that, over time and under the guidance of its mentor, the Occult and especially the hedonistic aspects came to dominate over the political and subversive intent, with the *raisons d'etat* of blackmail and persuasion, of recruiting

useful, respectable, people thus lost. Hence, while I still considered, then and for quite some time afterwards, that the basic idea of such a subversive group, such a honeytrap, was sound, I gradually lost interest in this particular immoral honeytrap project until another spell in prison for an assortment of offences took me away from Leeds and my life as a violent neo-nazi activist [...]

I had occasion, during the 1980's, to renew my association not only with some old C88 comrades but also with the mentor of that Occult honeytrap when, after of lapse of many years, I became involved again in neo-nazi politics and revived my project of using clandestine recruitment for 'the cause'. By this time, that Occult group had developed some useful contacts, especially in the academic world, so some friendly co-operation between us was agreed; a co-operation which continued, sporadically, until just before my conversion to Islam in 1998.

This clandestine recruitment of mine was for a small National-Socialist cadre which went by a variety of names, beginning with 'G7' (soon abandoned), then *The White Wolves* (c. 1993), and finally the *Aryan Resistance Movement* aka Aryan Liberation Army [qv. Part Five for details].

However, while some of these Occult contacts were, given their professions, occasionally useful 'to the cause' and to 'our people', by 1997 I had come to the conclusion that the problems such association with Occultism and occultists caused far outweighed the subversive advantages; a conclusion which led me to re-write and re-issue a much earlier article of mine entitled *Occultism and National-Socialism*, and which revised article was subsequently published in the compilation *Cosmic Reich* by Renaissance Press of New Zealand. As I wrote in that article - "National-Socialism and Occultism are fundamentally, and irretrievably, incompatible and opposed to each other."

By the Summer of 1998 I had abandoned not only such co-operation and contacts with such Occult groups but also such clandestine recruitment on behalf of National-Socialism, concentrating instead on my Reichsfolk group and my 'revised' non-racist version of National-Socialism which I called 'ethical National-Socialism'. Later still, following my conversion to Islam, I was to reject even this version of National-Socialism."

This explains many things, including early occult articles with my name - not the name 'Anton Long' - in zines such as *The Lamp of Thoth*, and the early version of *Copula cum Daemone* (which in fact was about the birth of Adolf Hitler). One question Senholt does not ask is why both my name and the name Anton Long occur on the same early texts, with the simple answer being that there were two different people, one of whom (me) ceased all involvement with such occult honeytraps in 1998.

(2) My time as a Christian monk and my writings praising Catholicism in particular and Christianity in general.

This does not fit in with the claim of me being a life-long 'devotee of extreme ideologies' or being a satanist, so it is ignored. No attempt was made to use primary sources - to talk to people who knew me as monk and who could recount my life then, and my autobiography *Myngath* where I recount my time as a monk.

No mention is made of my many articles in which I praise Catholicism or refer to it in a positive way. For example, my mention of the numinosity of the Latin Tridentine Mass [qv. *Concerning The Nature of Religion and The Nature of The Numinous Way*] and of the sacrament of confession. As I wrote in *Soli Deo Gloria:*

> "It is my personal opinion that traditional Catholicism, with its Tridentine Mass and its particular conservative traditions, was a somewhat better, more harmonious, expression of the numinous (a necessary and relevant expression of the numinous), than both Protestantism and the reforms introduced by the Second Ecumenical Council of the Vatican, and which reforms served only to undermine the numinous, to untwist the threads that held together its 'hidden soul of harmony'."

There is also the small matter of me being married in Church in accordance with the Christian ceremony of marriage. And the small matter of writings of mine such as *Pathei-Mathos - A Path To Humility.*

(3) My article *Occultism and National-Socialism* - written in the 1980's and republished in the 1990's and again around 2006 - and in which I denounced occultism, is ignored.

(4) My writings about National Socialism and Islam - spanning some three decades - are for the most part ignored, except when they are adduced to show I, as a nazi or as a Muslim, incited violence and possibly terrorism. Are they ignored because they in their quantity and content reveal they were written by someone who was at the time of their writing a dedicated neo-nazi and then a dedicated Muslim, and which dedication to such causes most certainly precludes being some sort of sinister person who was just using those causes for his own satanic ends?

In addition, and importantly, what are also overlooked are:

> (a) The very real threat of being imprisoned for some of those writings - something surely only a genuine fanatic, a believer, would be prepared to do.

> (b) My decades of political activism on behalf of National-Socialism, my two terms of imprisonment resulting from such activities, and my involvement with the paramilitary group Column 88. Which long-term activities over some thirty years, which imprisonment, and which paramilitary involvement surely indicate an inner - a rather fanatical - dedication to that cause.

> (c) My travels, as a Muslim, to certain lands, the talks I gave to and the discussions I had with Muslims [8], and my regular attendance at Mosques to pray with other Muslims, which would indicate someone

who was, during those years, committed to that Way of Life.

(5) My semi-autobiographical poetry [9], my published correspondence, and my ethical philosophy of The Numinous Way/philosophy of pathei-mathos, are completely ignored. Why are these voluminous writings and these ideas of mine ignored? Because they honestly reveal the thoughts and feelings and ideas and experiences and (importantly) the failings of someone so different from a satanist that they have to be ignored.

(6) My years of interior ethical and philosophical struggle to reform, to change, myself - documented in hundreds of letters, essays, poems, especially after the suicide of my fiancée in 2006 - are completely ignored. Why? Because they do not fit in with the idea, with the theory, of me being 'a deceitful, manipulative, sinister trickster', the archetypal satanist.[10]

It seems, therefore, that *some* of the facts of my life have been interpreted in order to fit a theory regarding some posited and ideal ONA member, with this interpreted ONA life - with inconvenient facts and circumstances conveniently omitted or ignored - then being held up as proof that I am Anton Long, since this truncated, re-interpreted, life of mine allegedly seems to fit in with the person Anton Long is alleged to be or is said to be according to his satanist writings or according to what some anonymous person has written on the World Wide Web.

In essence, there are no proofs presented in the thesis, with many aspects of my life omitted and with no mention, let alone analysis, of those voluminous writings of mine which portray a person almost the exact opposite of a satanist.

As one person wrote in respect of the rumour, the allegation, and the claim, that I am the pseudonymous Anton Long,

> "We basically have a choice between: (i) believing Myatt is an
> astonishingly diabolical, duplicitous, creative, polymathical genius
> who over four decades has been playing 'sinister games' and who has
> not deviated from his youthful sinister cunning plan, and which
> diabolical genius makes the likes of Crowley and LaVey (and everyone
> else associated with modern Satanism and the 'left hand path') seem
> pathetic and mundane; or (ii) assuming Myatt has spent most of his
> adult life as a covert servant of the British state; or (iii) accepting that
> Myatt has lived a quite adventurous (but not an exceptionally
> amazing) life, has made mistakes, has suffered a personal tragedy, and
> has learned from and been changed by his experiences and by that
> tragedy [...]
>
> Which of [these] three scenarios is therefore the most plausible?
> Which offers the most simple, the most rational, explanation for
> Myatt's peregrinations? Which require the pomp of conspiracy theory,

and which involve superfluous causes, and (sometimes bizarre, sometimes astonishing) ad hoc assumptions and claims?" [11]

Conclusion

In respect of allegations about involvement with satanism and 'being Anton Long' - and in respect of those who manufacture and propagate them - my own experience, my pathei-mathos, manifest in my philosophy of Pathei-Mathos, leads me to two conclusions. My first conclusion is that the research done by some modern authors and even some academics - whose works are published by reputable publishers or quoted by others engaged in academic research - is inadequate and does not meet the taxing criteria of scholarship. Thus these works are unreliable; they have no gravitas, no worth - in terms of learning - for the sagacious.

My second conclusion is that most if not all modern Media that concern themselves with the deeds and lives of individuals – from un-scholarly books and essays, to newspapers, to television news programs and political documentaries, to magazines, to the World Wide Web – are by their very impersonal and mass-media nature unethical. Why? Because they are un-numinous, and encourage and often embody hubris, being as they are the realm of personal opinions, hasty judgement, and misapprehension, and the abode of those for whom 'a story' or some personal/political agenda/prejudice or 'their career' or some unethical un-numinous abstraction (such as 'the public interest') come before honour, empathy, and the reasoned judgement of a personal knowing that has extended over a lengthy period of causal Time and/or been based on an extended period of scholarly research.

A corollary is that those who use such Media, and/or unscholarly books/essays, as sources of allegedly reliable information, as a guide, as *a* or as *the* basis for their judgement about and knowledge of someone or some many, are being unfair and uncultured because lacking in the following necessary virtues: (1) a reasoned, balanced, and thus ethical, judgement; (2) the empathy of manifold direct personal contacts; and (3) a scholarly research and/or a personal knowing extending over many years. Virtues which are the genesis of a genuine understanding of, and thence an unbiased knowledge of, another human being; and virtues which rapid, impersonal, mass means of modern communication actively discourage and which virtues are seldom, it seems, cultivated and employed by those involved with and who use and who rely on such modern means for information.

Quite simply it is matter of honour. Of personal knowing. As I mentioned above, the traditional gentlemanly and ladylike virtues and their cultivation are no longer the standard which individuals are expected to aspire to and to uphold. Thus I do not expect the plethora of rumours and allegations about me to suddenly cease, although I admit I do and perhaps naively nurture a vague hope that what I have written here may cause a few individuals to reconsider the veracity of such rumours and allegations.

As for who and what I really am, I can only suggest the curious read such writings of mine as the following: (a) *One Vagabond In Exile From The Gods;* (b) *Religion, Empathy, and Pathei-Mathos;* and (c) *Understanding and Rejecting Extremism.*

Notes:

[1] Many people seem to rely on four items in respect of accusations of occult involvement. These items are: (1) an article published in 1998 in the Searchlight magazine entitled *The Most Evil Nazi in Britain;* (2) a 2009 thesis by Senholt entitled *Political Esotericism & the convergence of Radical Islam, Satanism and National Socialism in the Order of the Nine Angles;* (3) a chapter in Nicholas Goodrick-Clarke's book *Black Sun: Aryan Cults, Esoteric Nazism and the Politics of Identity* (published in 2001); and (4) a 1974 interview I allegedly gave to a reporter.

(a) In respect of the Senholt, see the section in this article subtitled *The Logical Fallacy of Incomplete Evidence - A Case Study.*

(b) In respect of Goodrick-Clarke, his identification of me, in his book, as 'Anton Long' is solely based on his claim that I was the author of a manuscript entitled *Diablerie, Revelations of a Satanist* the only known copy of which is in the British Library. No evidence, no sources, are provided for this claim - this assumption. No evidences or sources are given for his other claims about me, such as that "the ONA was founded by David Myatt" or that I was "a long time devotee of satanism."

In addition, Goodrick-Clarke never bothered to contact me regarding these claims of his, and the first thing I knew about them was when the book was published. Had he contacted me, then, I would have been in a position to supply him with the unpublished autobiographical MS that the plagiarist had purloined and used as the source for that fanciful work of fiction entitled *Diablerie.* An unpublished autobiographical MS that I circulated to a few friends, and a few 'interested parties', in the 1980's when I was engaged in writing *The Logic of History* from which the text *Vindex, The Destiny of the West* (published in 1984) derived. One of 'the interested parties' was the publisher of *Vindex, The Destiny of the West* who subsequently published some other pro-NS works of mine. An interesting overview of Diablerie is given in the 2012 e-text *A Sceptics Review of Diablerie*, by R. Parker.

It is interesting and - to me - relevant that among the many errors of Goodrick-Clarke are the following:
i) I was not born in 1952, as he claimed.
ii) I first met Colin Jordan in 1968, not 1969 as he claimed.
iii) My two terms of imprisonment for political offences were not both for six months, as he claimed.
iv) Morrison was never 'my follower' as Goodrick-Clarke claimed (Eddy was never anyone's follower).
v) Morrison's first name is Eddy, not Eddie as Goodrick-Clarke claimed.
vi) The Occult lady that 'Anton Long' met in the early 1970's did not 'lead the ONA' as Goodrick-Clark claimed, but rather the Camlad association, with the ONA being founded and then led by Anton Long himself following his meeting with that lady.
vii) He mentions a certain Wulstram Tedder whom he claims was a former aide of Colin Jordan during the old NSM days, whereas 'W Tedder' was one of the noms-de-plume I used, for instance when writing for John Tyndall's *Spearhead* magazine in the 1980's.

It also interesting that Goodrick-Clarke was ignorant of - or did not bother to discover - many documented things about me during the late 1960's and the early 1970's, such as my arrest by the Yorkshire Regional Crime Squad for organizing a gang of thieves. Instead, the often fictitious account he gives of 'my life' during that time is almost entirely taken from the fictional Diablerie manuscript

Such errors, and the lack of evidence to support his assumptions about me, really say all that needs to be said about this particular 'source'.

Interestingly (perhaps) another fanciful work of fiction, similar to *Diablerie*, and purporting to be yet another autobiography by 'Anton Long' seems to have been recently written by someone, possibly for financial gain resulting from selling it at some silly price to collectors of rare Occult memorabilia. The bulk of this new fictional 'autobiography' consists of an early (now out of date) edition of *Myngath* to which various fictional autobiographical stories and 'sinister' incidents and diatribes have been added in line with what might be expected from a mythical 'Anton Long'. Given that the majority of these autobiographical stories in this so-called *Bealuwes Gast* are quite risible and fanciful (and not fundamentally satanic at all), and given that the 'sinister diatribes' seem to have been cut-and-pasted from various internet articles attributed to those who over the years have used the nom-de-plume Anton Long, it seems unlikely that this forgery will ever be taken seriously by anyone. I mean - and to name just one risible example - who can take seriously a 'clockwork orange cult' and the wearing of white lab coats to boot...

Since this *Bealuwes Gast* also contains certain autobiographical information contained in private correspondence (e-mails) sent by me to a certain correspondent in 2009, I believe I know the identity of the author, or at least the identity of the person who supplied that private information to the author.

(c) In respect of the 1974 'interview', I reproduce a comment I made in part one of my *Autobiographical Notes*, first published in 2001:

" The journalist promised to let me read his final copy before it was published – a condition I had specified before giving the interview – and several photographs of me were taken, with him suggesting I hold something to do with the Occult, since he had noticed I had a collection of horror, and Occult, fiction (most of which in fact were given or loaned to me by Eddy Morrison). Perhaps foolishly, I agreed, holding up some Occult thingy which Joe Short had given to me a few days before. Our conversation lasted for about half an hour, during which the journalist took a few notes (it was not recorded).

I assumed that he would simply recount what I had said. Of course he neither showed me the article before publication, nor printed what I said, except for one short sentence about causing chaos. The journalist also made some rather silly allegations about animal sacrifice, which were investigated at the time by both the Police and the RSPCA whose conclusion was that they were fabrications concocted by the journalist, and perhaps, as I concluded, to get his name on the front page of the newspaper and sell more copies.

What surprised me (and to be honest, upset me, for a while), after this interview, was how so many people believed everything the journalist had written, without bothering to ask me for my side of the story. As if just because something was printed in some newspaper or other then "it must be true" or – as the cliché of mundanes goes: "there is no smoke without fire." And it was then that I learnt several valuable lessons: just how easily people can be manipulated, just how dishonest and conniving (and thus dishonourable) some journalists seemed to be, by nature; and just how powerful the established Media was, able make or break a person's reputation."

(d) In respect of the 1998 *Searchlight* item, I reproduce here a rather polemical item written by me, the fanatic, in 1998 (during my extremist decades) just before my conversion to Islam and privately circulated to the few members of Reichsfolk. The item was subsequently re-issued - with some amendments and alterations made by Richard Stirling - in 2003 as a confidential supplement to the *Reichsfolk Situation Report* of that year.

"Not once, in the past thirty years, has anyone provided any evidence of my alleged involvement with the Order of Nine Angles or with Satanism in general [...]

All *Searchlight* has ever done is make unsubstantiated allegations [...]

One of the unsubstantiated allegations of the *Searchlight* crowd is that I was a friend of someone called Vik Norris – something they blandly stated in their alleged 'expose' of me, under the headline *The Most Evil Nazi in Britain*, in the April 1998 issue of *Searchlight* magazine. No evidence for this allegation was presented then, or subsequently.

Indeed, the article simply contains bland assertions by them about me and Satanism with no evidence presented to support such assertions. For example: (1) they stated that the ONA was "formed by Myatt himself in the early 1980's" but offer no proof for this claim of theirs; (2) they write about "Myatt and his satanic friends" yet never name these alleged 'satanic' friends or provide any proof of involvement by any of my friends with Satanism; (3) they claim that "within days of being investigated", the ONA withdrew its material from the Internet and that I had shaved off my beard in an attempt to disguise myself, with yet again no evidence being provided for these allegations, which were patently untrue, as anyone could have verified at the time by searching the Internet, calling on me at my home or place of work or asking those with whom I worked.

Unsurprisingly, many people over the years have – for personal or political reasons – referenced this *Searchlight* article as 'proof' of my alleged involvement, when anyone of any sagacity on reading that and similar articles about me can rationally deduce that it and other such articles are merely malicious propaganda designed to discredit, but worded in such a dishonourable way that even were one to sue the authors for libel in a British civil court (assuming one had the money to do so) there would be no guarantee of success – a legalistic tactic such dishonourable journalists often rely on when they peddle their lies and make their malicious accusations.

As for me, I have never bothered to have recourse to civil law, and established Courts, to sue those making libellous allegations about me quite simply because the only law I believe in and strive to uphold is the law of personal honour. Given that I have challenged two journalists, according to the law of personal honour, to a duel with deadly weapons for making such malicious allegations, and given that they did not have the honour to accept this challenge or issue an apology in lieu of fighting a duel, I consider my honour vindicated and their own dishonourable character proven."

[2] The completed BBC programme was broadcast, as a 'Panorama Special' entitled The Nailbomber, on the 30th June, 2000. Nick Lowles, who at the time was working for *Searchlight*, was listed as the associate producer.

[3] The recent writings of mine include the compilation *Understanding and Rejecting Extremism*, as well as voluminous essays about The Numinous Way/The Way of Pathei-Mathos, and which mystical Way of Life is one of compassion, empathy, humility, gentleness, and love.

As I wrote in *Letter To My Undiscovered Self,*

"The honest, the obvious, truth was that I – and people like me or those who supported, followed, or were incited, inspired, by people like me – were and are the problem. That my, that our, alleged 'problems' (political/religious), were phantasmagoriacal; unreal; imagined; only projections based on, caused by, invented ideas that had no basis in reality, no basis in the simple reality of human beings. For the simple reality of most human beings is the need for simple, human, things: for personal love, for friendship, for a family, for a personal freedom, a security, a stability – a home, food, playfulness, a lack of danger – and for the dignity, the self-respect, that work provides.

But instead of love we, our selfish, our obsessed, our extremist kind, engendered hate. Instead of peace, we engendered struggle, conflict, killing. Instead of tolerance we engendered intolerance. Instead fairness and equality we engendered dishonour and discrimination. Instead of security we produced, we encouraged, revolution, violence, change.

The problem, the problems, lay inside us, in our kind, not in 'the world', not in others. We, our kind – we the pursuers of, the inventors of, abstractions, of ideals, of ideologies; we the selfish, the arrogant, the hubriatic, the fanatics, the obsessed – were and are the main causes of hate, of conflict, of suffering, of inhumanity, of violence. Century after century, millennia after millennia [...]

That it took me four decades, and the tragic death of two loved ones, to discover these simple truths surely reveals something about the person I was and about the extremisms I championed and fought for.

Now, I – with Sappho – not only say that,

> I love delicate softness:
> For me, love has brought the brightness
> And the beauty of the Sun ....

but also that a personal, mutual, love between two human beings is the most beautiful, the most sacred, the most important, the most human, thing in the world; and that the peace that most of us hope for, desire in our hearts, only requires us to be, to become, loving, kind, fair, empathic, compassionate, human beings. For that we just have to renounce our extremism, both inner and outer."

As I wrote in *Pathei-Mathos, Genesis of My Unknowing*:

"There are no excuses for my extremist past, for the suffering I caused to loved ones, to family, to friends, to those many more, those far more, 'unknown others' who were or who became the 'enemies' posited by some extremist ideology. No excuses because the extremism, the intolerance, the hatred, the violence, the inhumanity, the prejudice were mine; my responsibility, born from and expressive of my character; and because the discovery of, the learning of, the need to live, to regain, my humanity arose because of and from others and not because of me.

Thus what exposed my hubris - what for me broke down that certitude-of-knowing which extremism breeds and re-presents - was not something I did; not something I achieved; not something related to my character, my nature, at all. Instead, it was a gift offered to me by two others - the legacy left by their tragic early dying. That it took not one but two personal tragedies - some thirteen years apart - for me to accept and appreciate the gift of their love, their living, most surely reveals my failure, the hubris that for so long suffused me, and the strength and depth of my so lamentable extremism.

But the stark and uneasy truth is that I have no real, no definitive, answers for anyone, including myself. All I have now is a definite uncertitude of knowing, and certain feelings, some intuitions, some reflexions, a few certainly fallible suggestions arising mostly from reflexions concerning that, my lamentable, past, and thus - perhaps - just a scent, just a scent, of some understanding concerning some-things, perfumed as this understanding is with ineffable sadness."

[4] A revised and updated version of Senholt's thesis, under the title *Secret Identities in The Sinister Tradition*, is included in Per Faxneld & Jesper Petersen: *The Devil's Party - Satanism in Modernity*, Oxford University Press, 2012. International Standard Book Number 9780199779246

[5] For my view on Goodrick-Clarke, see footnote 1.

[6] The logical fallacy of incomplete evidence is when material concerning or assumptions about a particular matter are selected and presented to support a particular argument or conclusion, while other material or assumptions which do not support, which contradict, the chosen argument or conclusion are withheld or not discussed. In effect, selective evidence and/or selective argument are used in order to 'prove' a particular point, with such selectively being deliberate, or the result of fallacious reasoning or unscholarly research.

[7] Refer to footnote #51 of Kaplan's book *Nation and Race*. Northeastern University Press. 1998.

[8] Refer to Mark Weitzmann, *Anti-Semitism and Terrorism*, in Dienel, Hans-Liudger (ed), *Terrorism and the Internet: Threats, Target Groups, Deradicalisation Strategies*. NATO Science for Peace and Security Series, vol. 67. IOS Press, 2010. pp.16-17.

[9] The compilation *Relict* contains my selection of most of those poems, written between 1971 and 2012, that I feel are worth reading.

[10] Mention perhaps should also be made of my many writings about extremism, my extremist past, and my rejection of extremism, which post-date Senholt's thesis, and in which writings I have endeavoured to explore and understand the roots of both my extremism and of extremism itself. These writings include *The Development of The Numinous Way* (2012) and *Recuyle of the Philosophy of Pathei-Mathos* (2012).

Other such writings are included in the more recent *Understanding and Rejecting Extremism*.

Also of interest should be my seven-part retrospective and autobiographical text *The Ethos of Extremism, Some Reflexions on Politics and A Fanatical Life*, and which "personal reflexions on my forty years of extremism may be of interest to a few people, especially given that, as a result of experience, a pathei-mathos, I have come to reject racism, National-Socialism, hatred, and all forms of extremism, having developed a personal weltanschauung, a non-religious numinous way, centred around empathy, compassion, fairness, and love."

[11] Wright, Julie. *David Myatt, Satanism, and the Order of Nine Angles.* e-text, 2012. Revised 2016.